ocket

A POCKET STYLE MANUAL

Fourth Edition

Clarity

Grammar

Punctuation and Mechanics

Research

MLA, APA, *Chicago*

Usage/Grammatical Terms

Diana Hacker

Brief Contents

A POCKET STYLE MANUAL

Fourth Edition

Clarity

Grammar

Punctuation and Mechanics

Research

MLA, APA, *Chicago*

Usage / Grammatical Terms

Diana Hacker

Bedford / St. Martin's
Boston ◆ New York

For Bedford/St. Martin's
Senior Developmental Editor: Michelle M. Clark
Associate Editor: Caroline Thompson
Senior Production Editor: Anne Noonan
Senior Production Supervisor: Dennis Conroy
Marketing Manager: Richard Cadman
Editorial Assistant: Amy Hurd
Production Assistant: Kristen Merrill, Amy Derjue
Copyeditor: Barbara Flanagan
Text Design: Claire Seng-Niemoeller
Cover Design: Hannus Design Associates
Composition: Monotype Composition Company, Inc.
Printing and Binding: Quebecor World Kingsport

President: Joan E. Feinberg
Editorial Director: Denise B. Wydra
Editor in Chief: Karen S. Henry
Director of Marketing: Karen Melton Soeltz
Director of Editing, Design, and Production: Marcia Cohen
Managing Editor: Elizabeth M. Schaaf

Library of Congress Control Number: 2003107462

8   7   6   5   4   3
f   e   d   c   b   a

For *information, write:* Bedford/St. Martin's, 75 Arlington Street, Boston, MA 02116
(617-399-4000)

ISBN: 0-312-40684-3

How to use this book

A Pocket Style Manual is a quick reference for writers and researchers. As a writer, you can turn to it for advice on revising sentences for clarity, grammar, punctuation, and mechanics. As a researcher, you can refer to its tips on finding and evaluating sources and to its color-coded sections on writing MLA, APA, and *Chicago*-style papers.

Here are the book's reference features.

The brief or detailed contents. The brief table of contents inside the front cover will usually send you close to the information you're looking for. Occasionally you may want to consult the more detailed contents inside the back cover.

The index. If you aren't sure which topic to choose in one of the tables of contents, turn to the index at the back of the book. For example, you may not realize that the choice between *is* and *are* is a matter of subject-verb agreement. In that case simply look up "*is* vs. *are*" in the index and you will be directed to the pages you need.

Research sources. For advice on posing a research question and on finding and evaluating sources, turn to sections 25–27.

MLA, APA, and Chicago *papers.* Color-coded sections—red for MLA, teal for APA, and blue for *Chicago*—keep you focused on the type of research paper you are writing. Each section gives discipline-specific advice on supporting a thesis, avoiding plagiarism, and integrating and documenting sources. Directories to the documentation models are easy to find. Just look for the first of the pages marked with a color band.

The glossaries. When in doubt about the correct use of commonly confused or misused words (such as *affect* and *effect*), consult section 44, the glossary of usage. For brief definitions of grammatical terms such as *subordinate clause* and *participial phrase,* turn to section 45.

On the Web boxes. On the Web boxes in the book direct you to exercises, model papers, and other resources on the companion Web site.

A Pocket Style Manual is meant to be consulted as the need arises. Keep it on your desk—right next to your mouse pad—or tuck it into your backpack or jacket pocket and carry it with you as a ready resource.

Clarity

1   Tighten wordy sentences.

Long sentences are not necessarily wordy, nor are short
sentences always concise. A sentence is wordy if its
meaning can be conveyed in fewer words.

1a Redundancies

Redundancies such as *cooperate together, basic essentials,* and *true fact* are a common source of wordiness.
There is no need to say the same thing twice.

▶ Slaves were ~~portrayed or~~ stereotyped as lazy

   even though they were the main labor force of

   the South.

       works
▶ Daniel ~~is employed~~ at a software company ~~working~~

   as a marketing assistant.

Modifiers are redundant when their meanings are sug-
gested by other words in the sentence.

▶ Sylvia ~~very hurriedly~~ scribbled her name

   and phone number on the back of a greasy

   napkin.

1b Empty or inflated phrases

An empty word or phrase can be cut with little or no loss
of meaning. An inflated phrase can be reduced to a
word or two.

       O
▶ ~~In my opinion,~~ ~~o~~ur current immigration policy

   is misguided on several counts.

                      if
▶ We will file the appropriate forms ~~in the~~

   ~~event that~~ we cannot meet the deadline.

INFLATED	CONCISE
along the lines of	like
at the present time	now, currently
because of the fact that	because
by means of	by
due to the fact that	because
for the reason that	because
in order to	to
in spite of the fact that	although, though
in the event that	if
until such time as	until

1c Needlessly complex structures

In a rough draft, sentence structures are often more complex than they need to be.

► ~~There is~~ ^Aanother DVD ~~that~~ tells the story of Charles Darwin and introduces the theory of evolution.

► ~~It is imperative that~~ ^Aall police officers ^{must} follow strict procedures when apprehending a suspect.

► The CEO claimed that because of volatile market conditions she could not ~~make an~~ estimate ~~of~~ the company's future profits.

ON THE WEB ▶   dianahacker.com/pocket
► **Electronic grammar exercises**
  ► Clarity
    ► Wordy sentences

2 Prefer active verbs.

As a rule, active verbs express meaning more vigorously than their duller counterparts—forms of the verb *be* or verbs in the passive voice. Forms of *be* (*be, am, is, are, was, were, being,* and *been*) lack vigor because they convey no action. Passive verbs lack strength because their subjects receive the action instead of doing it.

Forms of *be* and passive verbs have legitimate uses, but if an active verb can convey your meaning as well, use it.

FORM OF *BE*	A surge of power *was* responsible for the destruction of the coolant pumps.
PASSIVE	The coolant pumps *were destroyed* by a surge of power.
ACTIVE	A surge of power *destroyed* the coolant pumps.

2a When to replace *be* verbs

Not every *be* verb needs replacing. The forms of *be* (*be, am, is, are, was, were, being, been*) work well when you want to link a subject to a noun that clearly renames it or to a vivid adjective that describes it: *Advertising is legalized lying. Great intellects are skeptical.*

If a *be* verb makes a sentence needlessly wordy, however, consider replacing it. Often a phrase following the verb will contain a word (such as *violation*) that suggests a more vigorous, active alternative (*violate*).

▶ Burying nuclear waste in Antarctica would ~~be in~~ *violate* ~~violation of~~ an international treaty.

▶ When Rosa Parks ~~was resistant to~~ *resisted* giving up her seat on the bus, she became a civil rights hero.

2b When to replace passive verbs

In the active voice, the subject of the sentence does the action; in the passive, the subject receives the action.

ACTIVE	The committee reached a decision.
PASSIVE	A decision was reached by the committee.

In passive sentences, the actor (in this case *committee*) frequently disappears from the sentence: *A decision was reached.*

In most cases, you will want to emphasize the actor, so you should use the active voice. To replace a passive verb with an active alternative, make the actor the subject of the sentence.

> *Lightning struck the transformer,*
> ▶ ~~The transformer was struck by lightning,~~
>   ^
>
> plunging us into darkness.

> *The settlers stripped the land of timber before realizing*
> ▶ ~~The land was stripped of timber before the settlers~~
>   ^
>
> ~~realized~~ the consequences of their actions.

The passive voice is appropriate when you wish to emphasize the receiver of the action or to minimize the importance of the actor. In the following sentence, for example, the writer wished to focus on the tobacco plants, not on the people spraying them: *As the time for harvest approaches, the tobacco plants are sprayed with a chemical to retard the growth of suckers.*

NOTE: In scientific writing, the passive voice properly puts the emphasis on the experiment or the process being described, not on the researcher: *The solution was heated to the boiling point, and then it was reduced in volume by 50 percent.*

ON THE WEB	dianahacker.com/pocket

▶ **Language Debates**
  ▶ Passive voice

ON THE WEB	dianahacker.com/pocket

▶ **Electronic grammar exercises**
  ▶ Clarity
    ▶ Active verbs

3 Balance parallel ideas.

If two or more ideas are parallel, they should be expressed in parallel grammatical form.

A kiss can be a comma, a question mark, or an exclamation point. —Mistinguett

This novel is not to be tossed lightly aside, but to be hurled with great force. —Dorothy Parker

3a Items in a series

Balance all items in a series by presenting them in parallel grammatical form.

▶ Cross-training involves a variety of exercises,
   lifting
   such as running, swimming, and weights.

▶ Abused children commonly exhibit one or

   more of the following symptoms: withdrawal,
   depression.
   rebelliousness, restlessness, and ~~they are~~

   ~~depressed.~~

▶ The winner of the gluttony contest swallowed six

   pancakes, slurped down a cream pie, gobbled
   devoured
   six waffles, and four pastries.

3b Paired ideas

When pairing ideas, underscore their connection by expressing them in similar grammatical form. Paired ideas are usually connected in one of three ways: (1) with a coordinating conjunction such as *and, but,* or *or;* (2) with a pair of correlative conjunctions such as *either . . . or, neither . . . nor, not only . . . but also,* or *whether . . . or;* or (3) with a word introducing a comparison, usually *than* or *as.*

▶ Many states are reducing property taxes for home

                             extending

  owners and ~~extend~~ financial aid in the form of tax
              ^

  credits to renters.

The coordinating conjunction *and* connects two verbs: *reducing . . . extending.*

▶ Thomas Edison was not only a prolific inventor but

  also ~~was~~ a successful entrepreneur.

The correlative conjunctions *not only . . . but also* connect two noun phrases: *a prolific inventor* and *a successful entrepreneur.*

                            to ground

▶ It is easier to speak in abstractions than ~~grounding~~

                                    ^

  one's thoughts in reality.

The comparative term *than* links two infinitive phrases: *to speak . . . to ground.*

NOTE: Repeat function words such as prepositions (*by, to*) and subordinating conjunctions (*that, because*) to make parallel ideas easier to grasp.

▶ Many hooked smokers try switching to a brand

                         to

  they find distasteful or a low tar and nicotine
                    ^

  cigarette.

| ON THE WEB | dianahacker.com/pocket |

▶ **Electronic grammar exercises**
   ▶ Clarity
      ▶ Parallelism

4   Add needed words.

Do not omit words necessary for grammatical or logical completeness. Readers need to see at a glance how the parts of a sentence are connected.

4a Words in compound structures

In compound structures, words are often omitted for economy: *Tom is a man who means what he says and [who] says what he means.* Such omissions are acceptable as long as the omitted word is common to both parts of the compound structure.

If the shorter version defies grammar or idiom because an omitted word is not common to both parts of the structure, the word must be put back in.

▶ Some of the regulars are acquaintances whom we
                      who
   see at work or live in our community.
            ^

   The word *who* must be included because *whom live in our community* is not grammatically correct.

               accepted
▶ Mayor Davis never has and never will accept a bribe.
                  ^

   Has . . . accept is not grammatically correct.

                        in
▶ Many South Pacific tribes still believe and live by
                        ^

   ancient laws.

   Believe . . . by is not idiomatic English.

4b The word *that*

Add the word *that* if there is any danger of misreading without it.

                        that
▶ Looking out the family room window, Sara saw her
                     ^

   favorite tree, which she had climbed so often as

   a child, was gone.

   Sara didn't see the tree; she saw that the tree was gone.

4c Words in comparisons

Comparisons should be between items that are alike. To compare unlike items is illogical and distracting.

> ► The women entering VMI can expect haircuts as
>   *those of*
> short as ~~the~~ male cadets.
>   ^

Haircuts must be compared with haircuts, not with cadets.

Comparisons should be complete enough so that readers will understand what is being compared.

INCOMPLETE Brand X is less salty.

COMPLETE Brand X is less salty than Brand Y.

Also, you should leave no ambiguity about meaning. In the following sentence, two interpretations are possible.

AMBIGUOUS Mr. Kelly helped me more than Sam.

CLEAR Mr. Kelly helped me more than he helped Sam.

CLEAR Mr. Kelly helped me more than Sam did.

ON THE WEB dianahacker.com/pocket

► **Electronic grammar exercises**
  ► Clarity
    ► Needed words

---

5 Eliminate confusing shifts.

5a Shifts in point of view

The point of view of a piece of writing is the perspective from which it is written: first person (*I* or *we*), second person (*you*), or third person (*he/she/it/one* or *they*). Writers who are having difficulty settling on an appropriate point of view sometimes shift confusingly from one to another. The solution is to choose a suitable perspective and then stay with it.

▶ One week our class met to practice rescuing a

                                     We

   victim trapped in a wrecked car. ~~You~~ were graded

      our   *our*

   on ~~your~~ speed and ~~your~~ skill.

   You need

▶ ~~One needs~~ a password and a credit card number to

   access this database. You will be billed at an

   hourly rate.

Shifts from the third-person singular to the third-person plural are especially common. (See also 12a.)

   Artists are

▶ ~~The artist is~~ often seen as a threat to society,

   especially when they refuse to conform to

   conventional standards of taste.

NOTE: The *I* (or *we*) point of view, which emphasizes the writer, is a good choice for writing based primarily on personal experience. The *you* point of view, which emphasizes the reader, works well for giving advice or explaining how to do something. The third-person point of view, which emphasizes the subject, is appropriate in most academic and professional writing.

5b Shifts in tense

Consistent verb tenses clearly establish the time of the actions being described. When a passage begins in one tense and then shifts without warning and for no reason to another, readers are distracted and confused.

▶ There was no way I could fight the current and

                                    jumped

   win. Just as I was losing hope, a stranger ~~jumps~~

                        swam

   off a passing boat and ~~swims~~ toward me.

Writers often shift verb tenses when writing about literature. The literary convention is to describe fictional events consistently in the present tense. (See p. 35.)

▶ The scarlet letter is a punishment sternly placed

                                                   is

   on Hester's breast by the community, and yet it ~~was~~

   an extremely fanciful and imaginative product of

   Hester's own needlework.

ON THE WEB   dianahacker.com/pocket

▶ **Electronic grammar exercises**
   ▶ Clarity
      ▶ Shifts

---

6 Untangle mixed constructions.

A mixed construction contains parts that do not sensibly fit together. The mismatch may be a matter of grammar or of logic.

6a Mixed grammar

A writer should not begin with one grammatical plan and then switch without warning to another.

      M
▶ ~~For~~ most drivers who have a blood alcohol concen-

   tration of .05 percent increase their risk of causing

   an accident.

The phrase beginning with *For* cannot serve as the subject of the sentence. If the phrase opens the sentence, it must be followed by a subject and a verb: *For most drivers who have a blood alcohol concentration of .05 percent, the risk of causing an accident is increased.*

▶ Although the United States is one of the wealthi-

   est nations in the world, ~~but~~ almost 20 percent of

   American children live in poverty.

The *Although* clause is subordinate, so it cannot be linked to an independent clause with the coordinating conjunction *but.*

6b Illogical connections

A sentence's subject and verb should make sense together.

▶ Under the revised plan, the elderly/~~who now~~ *the double personal exemption for*

~~receive a double personal exemption/~~ will be

abolished.

The exemption, not the elderly, will be abolished.

▶ Social workers decided that ~~Tiffany's welfare~~ *Tiffany*

would not be safe living with her mother.

Tiffany, not her welfare, may not be safe.

6c *is when, is where,* and *reason . . . is because* constructions

In formal English many readers object to *is when, is
where,* and *reason . . . is because* constructions on either
logical or grammatical grounds.

▶ Anorexia nervosa is ~~where people,~~ believing they *a disorder suffered by people who,*

are too fat, diet to the point of starvation.

Anorexia nervosa is a disorder, not a place.

▶ ~~The reason~~ I was late ~~is~~ because my motorcycle

broke down.

The writer might have replaced the word *because* with *that,*
but the preceding revision is more concise.

ON THE WEB ▶ dianahacker.com/pocket

▶ **Electronic grammar exercises**
  ▶ Clarity
    ▶ Mixed constructions

7 | # Repair misplaced and dangling modifiers.

Modifiers should point clearly to the words they modify. As a rule, related words should be kept together.

7a Misplaced words

The most commonly misplaced words are limiting modifiers such as *only, even, almost, nearly,* and *just.* They should appear in front of a verb only if they modify the verb: *At first I couldn't even touch my toes.* If they limit the meaning of some other word in the sentence, they should be placed in front of that word.

        only
▶ Lasers ~~only~~ destroy the target, leaving the

surrounding healthy tissue intact.

The limiting modifier *not* is frequently misplaced, suggesting a meaning the writer did not intend.

     not
▶ In 1860, all black southerners were ~~not~~ slaves.

The original sentence means that no black southerners were slaves. The revision makes the writer's real meaning clear.

7b Misplaced phrases and clauses

Although phrases and clauses can appear at some distance from the words they modify, make sure your meaning is clear. When phrases or clauses are oddly placed, absurd misreadings can result.

   On the walls
▶ ~~There~~ are many pictures of comedians who have

performed at Gavin's. ~~on the walls.~~

The comedians weren't performing on the walls; the pictures were on the walls.

         150-pound,
▶ The robber was described as a six-foot-tall man

with a mustache. ~~weighing 150 pounds.~~

The robber, not the mustache, weighed 150 pounds.

7c Dangling modifiers

A dangling modifier fails to refer logically to any word in the sentence. Dangling modifiers are usually introductory word groups that suggest but do not name an actor. When a sentence opens with such a modifier, readers expect the subject of the following clause to name the actor. If it doesn't, the modifier dangles.

DANGLING

Upon entering the doctor's office, a skeleton caught my attention.

This sentence suggests—absurdly—that the skeleton entered the doctor's office.

To repair a dangling modifier, you can revise the sentence in one of two ways:

1. Name the actor immediately following the introductory modifier or
2. turn the modifier into a word group that names the actor.

▶ Upon entering the doctor's office, a skeleton. *I noticed*
~~caught my attention.~~

▶ *As I entered*
~~Upon entering~~ the doctor's office, a skeleton caught my attention.

A dangling modifier cannot be repaired simply by moving it: *A skeleton caught my attention upon entering the doctor's office.* The sentence still suggests that the skeleton entered the doctor's office.

▶ *I was*
While working as a ranger in Everglades National Park, a Florida panther crossed the road in front of my truck one night.

The panther wasn't working as a ranger. The writer has revised the sentence by naming the actor (*I*) in the opening modifier.

► After completing seminary training, ~~woman's~~ access

     women have often been denied

   to the pulpit. ~~has often been denied.~~

The women (not their access to the pulpit) complete the training. The writer has revised the sentence by making *women* (not *women's access*) the subject.

ON THE WEB   dianahacker.com/pocket

► **Language Debates**
  ► Dangling modifiers

7d Split infinitives

An infinitive consists of *to* plus a verb: *to think, to dance.* When a modifier appears between its two parts, an infinitive is said to be "split": *to carefully balance.* If a split infinitive is awkward, move the modifier to another position in the sentence.

► Cardiologists encourage their patients to

                   more carefully.

   ~~more carefully~~ watch their cholesterol levels.

When a split infinitive is more natural and less awkward than alternative phrasing, most readers find it acceptable. *We decided to actually enforce the law* is a perfectly natural construction in English. *We decided actually to enforce the law* is not.

ON THE WEB   dianahacker.com/pocket

► **Language Debates**
  ► Split infinitives

ON THE WEB   dianahacker.com/pocket

► **Electronic grammar exercises**
  ► Clarity
    ► Misplaced and dangling modifiers

8   Provide some variety.

When a rough draft is filled with too many same-sounding sentences, try to inject some variety—as long as you can do so without sacrificing clarity or ease of reading.

8a   Combining choppy sentences

If a series of short sentences sounds choppy, consider combining some of them. Look for opportunities to tuck some of your ideas into subordinate clauses. Subordinate clauses, which contain subjects and verbs, begin with words like these: *after, although, because, before, if, since, that, unless, until, when, where, which,* and *who.*

▶ The executive committee was made up of super-
         who
stars/ ~~They~~ fought for leadership instead of
    ^

addressing the company's problems.

▶ We keep our use of insecticides, herbicides, and
                      because we
fungicides to a minimum/ ~~We~~ are concerned about
                   ^

the environment.

Also look for opportunities to tuck some of your ideas into phrases, word groups that lack subjects or verbs (or both).

▶ The Chesapeake and Ohio Canal, ~~is~~ a 184-mile
                         ^

waterway constructed in the 1800s/ ~~It~~ was a major
                        ^

source of transportation for goods during the

Civil War.

  Enveloped
▶ ~~Sister Consilio was enveloped~~ in a black robe with
 ^
                        Sister Consilio
only her face and hands visible/ ~~She~~ was an
                     ^

imposing figure.

At times it will make sense to combine short sentences by joining them with *and, but,* or *or.*

▶ Shore houses were flooded up to the first floor, *and*
^

Brandt's Lighthouse was swallowed by the sea.

CAUTION: Avoid stringing a series of sentences together with *and, but,* or *or.* For sentence variety, place some of the ideas in subordinate clauses or phrases.

When my
▶ ~~My~~ uncle noticed the frightened look on my face,
^

~~and~~ he told me that the dentures in the glass were

not real teeth.

▶ These particles, ~~are~~ known as "stealth liposomes,"
^

~~and they~~ can hide in the body for a long time

without detection.

8b Varying sentence openings

Most sentences in English begin with the subject, move to the verb, and continue to an object, with modifiers tucked in along the way or put at the end. For the most part, such sentences are fine. Put too many of them in a row, however, and they become monotonous.

Words, phrases, or clauses modifying the verb can often be inserted ahead of the subject.

Eventually a
▶ ~~A~~ few drops of sap ~~eventually~~ began to trickle into
^

the pail.

Just as we were heading to work, the
▶ ~~The~~ earthquake rumbled throughout the valley. ~~just~~
^   ^

~~as we were heading to work.~~

Participial phrases can frequently be moved to the beginning of a sentence without loss of clarity.

D
▶ ~~The university,~~ discouraged by the researchers'
                    ^
                          the university
apparent lack of progress, nearly withdrew funding
                                                  ^
for these prize-winning experiments.

NOTE: When you begin a sentence with a participial phrase, make sure that the subject of the sentence names the person or thing being described. If it doesn't, the phrase will dangle. (See 7c.)

ON THE WEB   dianahacker.com/pocket

▶ **Electronic grammar exercises**
  ▶ Clarity
    ▶ Sentence variety

---

9 Find an appropriate voice.

An appropriate voice is one that suits your subject, engages your audience, and conforms to the conventions of the genre in which you are writing. When in doubt about the conventions of a particular genre—lab reports, informal essays, research papers, business memos, and so on—look at models written by experts in the field.

In the academic, professional, and business worlds, three kinds of language are generally considered inappropriate: jargon, which sounds too pretentious; slang, which sounds too casual; and sexist or biased language, which offends many readers.

9a Jargon

Jargon is specialized language used among members of a trade, profession, or group. Use jargon only when readers will be familiar with it; even then, use it only when plain English will not do as well.

JARGON   For decades the indigenous body politic of South
          Africa attempted to negotiate legal enfranchise-
          ment without result.

REVISED   For decades the indigenous people of South
          Africa negotiated in vain for the right to vote.

Broadly defined, jargon includes puffed-up language designed more to impress readers than to inform them. Common examples in business, government, higher education, and the military are given in the following list, with plain English translations in parentheses.

commence (begin)	indicator (sign)
components (parts)	input (advice)
endeavor (try)	optimal (best)
exit (leave)	parameters (boundaries)
facilitate (help)	prior to (before)
factor (consideration, cause)	prioritize (set priorities)
finalize (finish)	utilize (use)
impact (v.) (affect)	viable (workable)

Sentences filled with jargon are hard to read, and they are often wordy as well.

> ► If managers ~~have adequate input from~~ *listen to* subordinates, they can ~~effectuate more viable~~ *make better* decisions.

> ► All ~~employees functioning in the capacity of~~ work-study students ~~are required to give evidence of~~ *must prove that they are currently enrolled.* ~~current enrollment.~~

9b Clichés

The pioneer who first announced that he had "slept like a log" no doubt amused his companions with a fresh and unlikely comparison. Today, however, that comparison is a cliché, a saying that has lost its dazzle from overuse. No longer can it surprise.

In your writing do not rely heavily on clichés. To see just how predictable clichés are, put your hand over the right-hand column below and then finish the phrases given on the left.

cool as a	cucumber
beat around	the bush
busy as a	bee, beaver
crystal	clear
light as a	feather
like a bull	in a china shop

playing with	fire
nutty as a	fruitcake
selling like	hotcakes
water under the	bridge
white as a	sheet, ghost
avoid clichés like the	plague

The cure for clichés is frequently simple: Just delete them. When this won't work, try adding some element of surprise. One student, for example, who had written that she had butterflies in her stomach, revised her cliché like this:

> If all of the action in my stomach is caused by butterflies, there must be a horde of them, with horseshoes on.

The image of butterflies wearing horseshoes is fresh and unlikely, not dully predictable like the original cliché.

ON THE WEB   dianahacker.com/pocket
▶ **Language Debates**
   ▶ Clichés

9c Slang

Slang is an informal and sometimes private vocabulary that expresses the solidarity of a group such as teenagers, rock musicians, or soccer fans. Although it does have a certain vitality, slang is a code that not everyone understands, and it is too informal for most written work.

                      a creative
▶ The new governor is ~~an out-of-the-box~~ thinker.

9d Sexist language

Sexist language is language that stereotypes or demeans men or women, usually women. Such language arises from stereotypical thinking, from traditional pronoun use, and from words used to refer indefinitely to both sexes.

Stereotypical thinking.   In your writing, avoid referring to any one profession as exclusively male or exclusively female (such as referring to nurses in general as females). Also avoid using different conventions when identifying women and men (such as giving a woman's marital status but not a man's).

▶ All executives' ~~wives~~ *spouses* are invited to the picnic.

▶ Boris Stotsky, attorney, and ~~Mrs.~~ Cynthia Jones, *graphic designer,* ~~mother of three,~~ are running for city council.

The pronouns he *and* him.   Traditionally, *he, him,* and *his* were used to refer indefinitely to persons of either sex: *A journalist is stimulated by his deadline.* You can avoid such usage in one of three ways: substitute a pair of pronouns (*he or she, his or her*); reword in the plural; or revise the sentence to avoid the problem.

▶ A journalist is stimulated by his *or her* deadline.

▶ ~~A journalist is~~ *Journalists are* stimulated by ~~his deadline.~~ *their deadlines.*

▶ A journalist is stimulated by ~~his~~ *a* deadline.

man *words.*   Like *he* and *his,* the nouns *man* and *men* and related words containing them were once used indefinitely to refer to persons of either sex. Use gender-neutral terms instead.

INAPPROPRIATE	APPROPRIATE
chairman	chairperson, chair
congressman	representative, legislator
fireman	firefighter
mailman	mail carrier, postal worker
mankind	people, humans
to man	to operate, to staff
weatherman	meteorologist, forecaster
workman	worker, laborer

ON THE WEB   dianahacker.com/pocket
▶ **Language Debates**
   ▶ Sexist language

ON THE WEB   dianahacker.com/pocket
► Electronic grammar exercises
   ► Clarity
      ► Sexist language

9e Offensive language

Obviously it is impolite to use offensive terms such as *Polack* or *redneck,* but offensive language can take more subtle forms. When describing groups of people, choose names that the groups currently use to describe themselves.

►   North Dakota takes its name from the ~~Indian~~ word
                                            Sioux

     meaning "friend" or "ally."

►   Many ~~Oriental~~ immigrants have recently settled in
          Asian

     our small town.

Avoid stereotyping a person or a group even if you believe your generalization to be positive.

►   It was no surprise that Greer, ~~a Chinese American,~~
                                   an excellent math and science student,

     was selected for the honors chemistry program.

Make subjects and verbs agree.

In the present tense, verbs agree with their subjects in number (singular or plural) and in person (first, second, or third). The present-tense ending -s is used on a verb if its subject is third-person singular; otherwise the verb takes no ending. Consider, for example, the present-tense forms of the verb *give*:

	SINGULAR	PLURAL
FIRST PERSON	I give	we give
SECOND PERSON	you give	you give
THIRD PERSON	he/she/it gives Yolanda gives	they give parents give

The verb *be* varies from this pattern, and unlike any other verb it has special forms in *both* the present and the past tense.

PRESENT-TENSE FORMS OF *BE*		PAST-TENSE FORMS OF *BE*	
I am	we are	I was	we were
you are	you are	you were	you were
he/she/it is	they are	he/she/it was	they were

Problems with subject-verb agreement tend to arise in certain tricky contexts, which are detailed in this section.

10a Words between subject and verb

Word groups often come between the subject and the verb. Such word groups, usually modifying the subject, may contain a noun that at first appears to be the subject. By mentally stripping away such modifiers, you can isolate the noun that is in fact the subject.

The *samples* on the tray in the lab *need* testing.

▶ High levels of air pollution damages the

respiratory tract.

The subject is *levels,* not *pollution.*

▶ The slaughter of pandas for their pelts ~~have~~ *has*

caused the panda population to decline drastically.

The subject is *slaughter*, not *pandas* or *pelts*.

NOTE: Phrases beginning with the prepositions *as well as, in addition to, accompanied by, together with,* and *along with* do not make a singular subject plural: *The governor, as well as his aide, was* [not *were*] *indicted.*

10b Subjects joined by *and*

Compound subjects joined by *and* are nearly always plural.

▶ Jill's natural ability and her desire to help others
have
~~has~~ led to a career in the ministry.

EXCEPTION: If the parts of the subject form a single unit, however, you may treat the subject as singular: *Bacon and eggs is my favorite breakfast.*

10c Subjects joined by *or* or *nor*

With compound subjects connected by *or* or *nor,* make the verb agree with the part of the subject nearer to the verb.

▶ If a relative or neighbor ~~are~~ *is* abusing a child,

notify the police.

▶ Neither the lab assistant nor the students ~~was~~ *were* able

to download the program.

10d Indefinite pronouns such as *someone*

Indefinite pronouns refer to nonspecific persons or things. Even though the following indefinite pronouns may seem to have plural meanings, treat them as singular in formal English: *anybody, anyone, each, either, everybody, everyone, everything, neither, no one, somebody, someone, something.*

> *favors*
> Nearly everyone on the panel ~~favor~~ the new budget.
> ^

> *has*
> Each of the furrows ~~have~~ been seeded.
> ^

A few indefinite pronouns (*all, any, none, some*) may be singular or plural depending on the noun or pronoun they refer to: *Some of the lemonade has disappeared. Some of the rocks were slippery. None of his advice makes sense. None of the eggs were broken.*

ON THE WEB dianahacker.com/pocket

> **Language Debates**
> > *none*

10e Collective nouns such as *jury*

Collective nouns such as *jury, committee, club, audience, crowd, class, troop, family*, and *couple* name a class or a group. In American English, collective nouns are usually treated as singular: They emphasize the group as a unit.

> *meets*
> The board of trustees ~~meet~~ in Denver on the first
> ^
>
> Tuesday of each month.

Occasionally, when there is some reason to draw attention to the individual members of the group, a collective noun may be treated as plural: *A young couple were arguing about politics while holding hands.* (Only individuals can argue and hold hands.)

NOTE: When units of measurement are used collectively, treat them as singular: *Three-fourths of the pie has been eaten.* When they refer to individual persons or things, treat them as plural: *One-fourth of the children were labeled "talented and gifted."*

10f Subject after verb

Verbs ordinarily follow subjects. When this normal order is reversed, it is easy to become confused.

> *are*
> ▶ Of particular concern ~~is~~ penicillin and tetracycline,
>   ^

antibiotics used to make animals more resistant

to disease.

The subject *penicillin and tetracycline* is plural.

The subject always follows the verb in sentences beginning with *There is* or *There are* (or *There was* or *There were*).

> *are*
> ▶ There ~~is~~ a small aquarium and an enormous
>   ^

terrarium in our biology lab.

The subject *aquarium and terrarium* is plural.

10g *who, which,* and *that*

Like most pronouns, the relative pronouns *who, which,* and *that* have antecedents, nouns or pronouns to which they refer. Relative pronouns used as subjects take verbs that agree with their antecedents.

Pick a stock that pays good dividends.

Constructions such as *one of the students who* [or *one of the things that*] cause problems for writers. Do not assume that the antecedent must be *one*. Instead, you should consider the logic of the sentence.

> ▶ Our ability to use language is one of the things
>   *set*
>   that ~~sets~~ us apart from animals.
>   ^

The antecedent of *that* is *things,* not *one*. Several things set us apart from animals.

When the word *only* comes before *one,* you are safe in assuming that *one* is the antecedent of the relative pronoun.

> ▶ SEACON is the only one of our war games that
>   *emphasizes*
>   ~~emphasize~~ scientific and technical issues.
>   ^

The antecedent of *that* is *one,* not *games.* Only one game emphasizes scientific and technical issues.

ON THE WEB   dianahacker.com/pocket

► **Language Debates**
    ► *one of those who* (or *that*)

10h Plural form, singular meaning

Words such as *athletics, economics, mathematics, physics, statistics, measles,* and *news* are usually singular, despite their plural form.

> ► Statistics ~~are~~ among the most difficult courses in
>   *is*
>
> our program.

EXCEPTION: When they describe separate items rather than a collective body of knowledge, words such as *athletics, mathematics,* and *statistics* are plural: *The statistics on school retention rates are impressive.*

10i Titles, company names, and words mentioned as words

Titles, company names, and words mentioned as words are singular.

> ►   *describes*
> *Lost Cities* ~~describe~~ the discoveries of many
>
> ancient civilizations.

> ►   *specializes*
> Delmonico Brothers ~~specialize~~ in organic produce
>
> and additive-free meats.

> ►   *is*
> *Controlled substances* ~~are~~ a euphemism for illegal
>
> drugs.

ON THE WEB   dianahacker.com/pocket

► **Electronic grammar exercises**
    ► Grammar
        ► Subject-verb agreement

11 Be alert to other problems with verbs.

The verb is the heart of the sentence, so it is important to get it right. Section 10 deals with the problem of subject-verb agreement. This section describes a few other potential problems with verbs.

11a Irregular verbs

For all regular verbs, the past-tense and past-participle forms are the same, ending in *-ed* or *-d*, so there is no danger of confusion. This is not true, however, for irregular verbs such as the following.

BASE FORM	PAST TENSE	PAST PARTICIPLE
begin	began	begun
fly	flew	flown
ride	rode	ridden

The past-tense form, which never has a helping verb, expresses action that occurred entirely in the past. The past participle is used with a helping verb—either with *has, have,* or *had* to form one of the perfect tenses or with *be, am, is, are, was, were, being,* or *been* to form the passive voice.

PAST TENSE   Last July, we *went* to Paris.

PAST PARTICIPLE   We have *gone* to Paris twice.

When you aren't sure which verb form to choose (*went* or *gone, began* or *begun,* and so on), consult the list that begins on page 30. Choose the past-tense form if your sentence doesn't have a helping verb; choose the past-participle form if it does.

▶ Yesterday we ~~seen~~ *saw* an unidentified flying object.

Because there is no helping verb, the past-tense form *saw* is required.

▶ By the end of the day, the stock market had ~~fell~~ *fallen*

two hundred points.

Because of the helping verb *had,* the past-participle form *fallen* is required.

Distinguishing between lie *and* lay.   Writers often confuse the forms of *lie* (meaning "to recline or rest on a surface") with *lay* (meaning "to put or place something"). The intransitive verb *lie* does not take a direct object: *The tax forms are lying on the coffee table.* The transitive verb *lay* takes a direct object: *Please lay the tax forms on the coffee table.*

In addition to confusing the meanings of *lie* and *lay*, writers are often unfamiliar with the standard English forms of these verbs. Their past-tense and past-participle forms are given in the list of common irregular verbs that begins on this page. The present participle of *lie* is *lying;* the present participle of *lay* is *laying.*

▶ Elizabeth was so exhausted that she ~~laid~~ down
                                      lay

for a nap.

> The past-tense form of *lie* ("to recline") is *lay.*

▶ The prosecutor ~~lay~~ the pistol on a table close to
                  laid

the jurors.

> The past-tense form of *lay* ("to place") is *laid.*

▶ Letters dating from the Civil War were ~~laying~~ in
                                         lying

the corner of the chest.

> The present participle of *lie* ("to rest on a surface") is *lying.*

ON THE WEB   dianahacker.com/pocket

▶ **Language Debates**
  ▶ *lie* versus *lay*

Common irregular verbs

BASE FORM	PAST TENSE	PAST PARTICIPLE
arise	arose	arisen
awake	awoke, awaked	awaked, awoke
be	was, were	been
beat	beat	beaten, beat
become	became	become
begin	began	begun
bend	bent	bent

BASE FORM	PAST TENSE	PAST PARTICIPLE
bite	bit	bitten, bit
blow	blew	blown
break	broke	broken
bring	brought	brought
build	built	built
burst	burst	burst
buy	bought	bought
catch	caught	caught
choose	chose	chosen
cling	clung	clung
come	came	come
cost	cost	cost
deal	dealt	dealt
dig	dug	dug
dive	dived, dove	dived
do	did	done
drag	dragged	dragged
draw	drew	drawn
dream	dreamed, dreamt	dreamed, dreamt
drink	drank	drunk
drive	drove	driven
eat	ate	eaten
fall	fell	fallen
fight	fought	fought
find	found	found
fly	flew	flown
forget	forgot	forgotten, forgot
freeze	froze	frozen
get	got	gotten, got
give	gave	given
go	went	gone
grow	grew	grown
hang (suspend)	hung	hung
hang (execute)	hanged	hanged
have	had	had
hear	heard	heard
hide	hid	hidden
hurt	hurt	hurt
keep	kept	kept
know	knew	known
lay (put)	laid	laid

BASE FORM	PAST TENSE	PAST PARTICIPLE
lead	led	led
lend	lent	lent
let (allow)	let	let
lie (recline)	lay	lain
lose	lost	lost
make	made	made
prove	proved	proved, proven
read	read	read
ride	rode	ridden
ring	rang	rung
rise (get up)	rose	risen
run	ran	run
say	said	said
see	saw	seen
send	sent	sent
set (place)	set	set
shake	shook	shaken
shoot	shot	shot
shrink	shrank	shrunk, shrunken
sing	sang	sung
sink	sank	sunk
sit (be seated)	sat	sat
slay	slew	slain
sleep	slept	slept
speak	spoke	spoken
spin	spun	spun
spring	sprang	sprung
stand	stood	stood
steal	stole	stolen
sting	stung	stung
strike	struck	struck, stricken
swear	swore	sworn
swim	swam	swum
swing	swung	swung
take	took	taken
teach	taught	taught
throw	threw	thrown
wake	woke, waked	waked, woken
wear	wore	worn
wring	wrung	wrung
write	wrote	written

11b Tense

Tenses indicate the time of an action in relation to the time of the speaking or writing about that action. The most common problem with tenses—shifting from one tense to another—is discussed in 5b. Other problems with tenses are detailed in this section, after the following survey of tenses.

Survey of tenses. Tenses are classified as present, past, and future, with simple, perfect, and progressive forms for each.

The simple tenses indicate relatively simple time relations. The present tense is used primarily for actions occurring at the time of the speaking or for actions occurring regularly. The past tense is used for actions completed in the past. The future tense is used for actions that will occur in the future. In the following table, the simple tenses are given for the regular verb *walk,* the irregular verb *ride,* and the highly irregular verb *be.*

PRESENT TENSE SINGULAR		PLURAL	
I	walk, ride, am	we	walk, ride, are
you	walk, ride, are	you	walk, ride, are
he/she/it	walks, rides, is	they	walk, ride, are

PAST TENSE SINGULAR		PLURAL	
I	walked, rode, was	we	walked, rode, were
you	walked, rode, were	you	walked, rode, were
he/she/it	walked, rode, was	they	walked, rode, were

FUTURE TENSE	
I, you, he/she/it, we, they	will walk, ride, be

More complex time relations are indicated by the perfect tenses. A verb in one of the perfect tenses (a form of *have* plus the past participle) expresses an action that was or will be completed at the time of another action.

PRESENT PERFECT	
I, you, we, they	have walked, ridden, been
he/she/it	has walked, ridden, been

PAST PERFECT	
I, you, he/she/it, we, they	had walked, ridden, been

FUTURE PERFECT	
I, you, he/she/it, we, they	will have walked, ridden, been

Each of the six tenses just mentioned has a progressive form used to express a continuing action. A progressive verb consists of a form of *be* followed by the present participle.

PRESENT PROGRESSIVE	
I	am walking, riding, being
he/she/it	is walking, riding, being
you, we, they	are walking, riding, being

PAST PROGRESSIVE	
I, he/she/it	was walking, riding, being
you, we, they	were walking, riding, being

FUTURE PROGRESSIVE	
I, you, he/she/it, we, they	will be walking, riding, being

PRESENT PERFECT PROGRESSIVE	
I, you, we, they	have been walking, riding, being
he/she/it	has been walking, riding, being

PAST PERFECT PROGRESSIVE	
I, you, he/she/it, we, they	had been walking, riding, being

FUTURE PERFECT PROGRESSIVE	
I, you, he/she/it, we, they	will have been walking, riding, being

Special uses of the present tense. Use the present tense when writing about literature or when expressing general truths.

> *is*
> ▶ Don Quixote, in Cervantes's novel, ~~was~~ an idealist
>   ^
>
>   ill suited for life in the real world.

> *orbits*
> ▶ Galileo taught that the earth ~~orbited~~ the sun.
>   ^

The past perfect tense. The past perfect tense is used for an action already completed by the time of another past action. This tense consists of a past participle preceded by *had* (*had worked, had gone*).

> ▶ We built our cabin forty feet above an abandoned
>   *had been*
>   quarry that ~~was~~ flooded in 1920 to create a lake.
>   ^

> ▶ When Hitler planned the Holocaust in 1941, did
>   *had*
>   he know that Himmler and the SS had mass
>   ^
>   murder in mind since 1938?

11c Mood

There are three moods in English: the *indicative,* used for facts, opinions, and questions; the *imperative,* used for orders or advice; and the *subjunctive,* used for wishes, conditions contrary to fact, and requests or recommendations. Of these three moods, the subjunctive is most likely to cause problems.

Use the subjunctive mood for wishes and in *if* clauses expressing conditions contrary to fact. The subjunctive in such cases is the past tense form of the verb; in the case of *be,* it is always *were* (not *was*), even if the subject is singular.

> I wish that Jamal *drove* more slowly late at night.

> If I *were* a member of Congress, I would vote for the bill.

Use the subjunctive mood in *that* clauses following verbs such as *ask, insist, recommend,* and *request.* The subjunctive in such cases is the base (or dictionary) form of the verb.

Dr. Chung insists that her students *be* on time.

We recommend that Dawson *file* form 1050 soon.

ON THE WEB   dianahacker.com/pocket

▶ **Electronic grammar exercises**
   ▶ Grammar
      ▶ Verbs

---

12   Use pronouns with care.

Pronouns are words that substitute for nouns: *he, it, them, her, me,* and so on. Four frequently encountered problems with pronouns are discussed in this section:

a.   pronoun-antecedent agreement (singular vs. plural)
b.   pronoun reference (clarity)
c.   case of personal pronouns (*I* vs. *me,* etc.)
d.   *who* vs. *whom*

ON THE WEB   dianahacker.com/pocket

▶ **Electronic grammar exercises**
   ▶ Grammar
      ▶ Pronoun-antecedent agreement
      ▶ Pronoun reference
      ▶ Pronoun case
      ▶ *who* vs. *whom*

12a Pronoun-antecedent agreement

The antecedent of a pronoun is the word the pronoun refers to. A pronoun and its antecedent agree when they are both singular or both plural.

SINGULAR   The *doctor* finished *her* rounds.

PLURAL   The *doctors* finished *their* rounds.

Writers are sometimes tempted to choose the plural pronoun *they* (or *their*) to refer to a singular antecedent. The temptation is greatest when the singular antecedent is an indefinite pronoun, a generic noun, or a collective noun.

Indefinite pronouns. Indefinite pronouns refer to non-specific persons or things. Even though some of the following indefinite pronouns may seem to have plural meanings, treat them as singular in formal English: *anybody, anyone, each, either, everybody, everyone, everything, neither, no one, someone, something.*

In this class *everyone* performs at *his or her* [not *their*] fitness level.

When *they* or *their* refers mistakenly to a singular antecedent such as *everyone,* you will usually have three options for revision:

1. Replace *they* with *he or she* (or *their* with *his or her*).
2. Make the singular antecedent plural.
3. Rewrite the sentence.

Because the *he or she* construction is wordy, often the second or third revision strategy is more effective.

▶ When someone has been drinking, ~~they are~~ *he or she is* more

   likely to speed.

▶ When ~~someone has~~ *drivers have* been drinking, they are more

   likely to speed.

▶ ~~When someone~~ *Someone who* has been drinking/ ~~they are~~ *is* more

   likely to speed.

NOTE: The traditional use of *he* (or *his*) to refer to persons of either sex is now widely considered sexist. (See p. 21.)

Generic nouns. A generic noun represents a typical member of a group, such as a student, or any member of a group, such as *any musician*. Although generic nouns may seem to have plural meanings, they are singular.

> Every *runner* must train rigorously if *he or she* wants [not *they want*] to excel.

When *they* or *their* refers mistakenly to a generic noun, you will usually have the same three revision options as for indefinite pronouns.

▶ A medical student must study hard if ~~they want~~ *he or she wants* to succeed.

▶ *Medical students* ~~A medical student~~ must study hard if they want to succeed.

▶ A medical student must study hard ~~if they want~~ to succeed.

Collective nouns.   Collective nouns such as *jury, committee, audience, crowd, family,* and *team* name a class or group. In American English, collective nouns are usually singular because they emphasize the group functioning as a unit.

> The planning *committee* granted *its* [not *their*] permission to build.

If the members of the group function individually, however, you may treat the noun as plural: *The family put their signatures on the document.* Or you might add a plural antecedent such as *members* to the sentence: *The members of the family put their signatures on the document.*

ON THE WEB   dianahacker.com/pocket

▶ **Language Debates**
  ▶ Pronoun–antecedent agreement

12b Pronoun reference

A pronoun should refer clearly to its antecedent. A pronoun's reference will be unclear if it is ambiguous, implied, vague, or indefinite.

Ambiguous reference. Ambiguous reference occurs when the pronoun could refer to two possible antecedents.

▶ When Aunt Harriet put ~~the cake~~ *it* on the table, ~~it~~ *the cake*
collapsed.

▶ Tom told James, *"You have* ~~that he had~~ won the lottery.*"*

What collapsed—the cake or the table? Who won the lottery—Tom or James? The revisions eliminate the ambiguity.

Implied reference. A pronoun must refer to a specific antecedent, not to a word that is implied but not actually stated.

▶ After braiding Ann's hair, Sue decorated ~~them~~ *the braids* with
ribbons.

Vague reference of this, that, *or* which. The pronouns *this, that,* and *which* should not refer vaguely to earlier word groups or ideas. These pronouns should refer to specific antecedents. When a pronoun's reference is too vague, either replace the pronoun with a noun or supply an antecedent to which the pronoun clearly refers.

▶ More and more often, especially in large cities, we
are finding ourselves victims of serious crimes. We
learn to accept ~~this~~ *our fate* with minor complaints.

▶ Romeo and Juliet were both too young to have
acquired much wisdom, *a fact* which accounts for
their rash actions.

Indefinite reference of they, it, *or* you.   The pronoun *they* should refer to a specific antecedent. Do not use *they* to refer indefinitely to persons who have not been specifically mentioned.

> *Congress*
> ▶ ~~They~~ shut down all government agencies for more
>   ^
>
>   than a month until the budget crisis was resolved.

The word *it* should not be used indefinitely in constructions such as "In the article it says that. . . ."

> *The*
> ▶ ~~In the~~ encyclopedia ~~it~~ states that male moths
>   ^
>
>   can smell female moths from several miles
>
>   away.

The pronoun *you* is appropriate when the writer is addressing the reader directly: *Once you have kneaded the dough, let it rise in a warm place.* Except in informal contexts, however, the indefinite *you* (meaning "anyone in general") is inappropriate.

> ▶ Ms. Pickersgill's *Guide to Etiquette* stipulates that
>   *guests*
>   ~~you~~ should not arrive at a party too early or
>   ^
>
>   leave too late.

ON THE WEB	dianahacker.com/pocket
▶ **Language Debates**	
▶ *you*	

12c Case of personal pronouns (*I* vs. *me,* etc.)

The personal pronouns in the following list change what is known as case form according to their grammatical function in a sentence. Pronouns functioning as subjects or subject complements appear in the *subjective* case; those functioning as objects appear in the *objective* case; and those functioning as possessives appear in the *possessive* case.

SUBJECTIVE CASE	OBJECTIVE CASE	POSSESSIVE CASE
I	me	my
we	us	our
you	you	your
he/she/it	him/her/it	his/her/its
they	them	their

For the most part, you know how to use these forms correctly, but certain structures may tempt you to choose the wrong pronoun.

Compound word groups. When a subject or object appears as part of a compound structure, you may occasionally become confused. To test for the correct pronoun, mentally strip away all of the compound structure except the pronoun in question.

▶ While diving for pearls, Ikiko and ~~her~~ *she* found a

treasure chest full of gold bars.

Ikiko and she is the subject of the verb *found.* Strip away the words *Ikiko and* to test for the correct pronoun: *she found* [not *her found*].

▶ The most traumatic experience for her father and
~~I~~ *me* occurred long after her operation.

Her father and me is the object of the preposition *for.* Strip away the words *her father and* to test for the correct pronoun: *for me* [not *for I*].

When in doubt about the correct pronoun, some writers try to evade the choice by using a reflexive pronoun such as *myself.* Such evasions are nonstandard, even though they are used by some educated persons.

▶ The Egyptian cab driver gave my husband and
~~myself~~ *me* some good tips on traveling in North Africa.

My husband and me is the indirect object of the verb *gave.*

ON THE WEB   dianahacker.com/pocket

▶ **Language Debates**
  ▶ *myself*

Subject complements. Use subjective-case pronouns for subject complements, which rename or describe the subject and usually follow *be, am, is, are, was, were, being,* or *been.*

▶ During the Lindbergh trial, Bruno Hauptmann repeatedly denied that the kidnapper was ~~him.~~ *he.*

> If *kidnapper was he* seems too stilted, rewrite the sentence: *During the Lindbergh trial, Bruno Hauptmann repeatedly denied that he was the kidnapper.*

Appositives. Appositives, noun phrases that rename nouns or pronouns, have the same function as the words they rename. To test for the correct pronoun, mentally strip away the words that the appositive renames.

▶ The chief strategists, Dr. Bell and ~~me,~~ *I,* could not agree on a plan.

> The appositive *Dr. Bell and I* renames the subject, *strategists.* Test: *I could not agree on a plan* [not *me could not agree on a plan*].

▶ The reporter interviewed only two witnesses, the shopkeeper and ~~I.~~ *me.*

> The appositive *the shopkeeper and me* renames the direct object, *witnesses.* Test: *interviewed me* [not *interviewed I*].

We or us before a noun. When deciding whether *we* or *us* should precede a noun, choose the pronoun that would be appropriate if the noun were omitted.

▶ *We* ~~Us~~ tenants would rather fight than move.

> Test: *We would rather fight* [not *Us would rather fight*].

▶ Management is short-changing ~~we~~ *us* tenants.

> Test: *Management is short-changing us* [not *Management is short-changing we*].

Pronoun after than *or* as. Sentence parts, usually verbs, are often omitted in comparisons beginning with *than* or *as*. To test for the correct pronoun, finish the sentence.

> My husband is six years older than ~~me.~~ *I.*

Test: *than I* [*am*].

> We respected no other candidate in the election as much as ~~she.~~ *her.*

Test: *as* [*we respected*] *her.*

Pronoun before or after an infinitive. An infinitive is the word *to* followed by a verb. Both subjects and objects of infinitives take the objective case.

> Ms. Wilson asked John and ~~I~~ *me* to drive the senator and ~~she~~ *her* to the airport.

John and me is the subject and *senator and her* is the object of the infinitive *to drive*.

Pronoun or noun before a gerund. If a pronoun modifies a gerund, use the possessive case: *my, our, your, his/her/its, their*. A gerund is a verb form ending in *-ing* that functions as a noun.

> The chances against ~~you~~ *your* being hit by lightning are about two million to one.

Nouns as well as pronouns may modify gerunds. To form the possessive case of a noun, use an apostrophe and an *-s* (*a victim's suffering*) or just an apostrophe (*victims' suffering*). (See 19a.)

> The old order in France paid a high price for the ~~aristocracy~~ *aristocracy's* exploiting the lower classes.

12d *who* or *whom*

Who, a subjective-case pronoun, can be used only for subjects and subject complements. *Whom,* an objective-case pronoun, can be used only for objects. The words *who* and *whom* appear primarily in subordinate clauses or in questions.

In subordinate clauses.   When deciding whether to use *who* or *whom* in a subordinate clause, check for the word's function within the clause.

> *whoever*
> ► He tells that story to ~~whomever~~ will listen.

> *Whoever* is the subject of *will listen.* The entire subordinate clause *whoever will listen* is the object of the preposition *to.*

> *whom*
> ► You will work with our senior engineers, ~~who~~ you
>
> will meet later.

> *Whom* is the direct object of the verb *will meet.* This becomes clear if you restructure the clause: *you will meet whom later.*

In questions.   When deciding whether to use *who* or *whom* in a question, check for the word's function within the question.

> *Who*
> ► ~~Whom~~ was accused of receiving money from
>
> the Mafia?

> *Who* is the subject of the verb *was accused.*

> *Whom*
> ► ~~Who~~ did the Democratic Party nominate in 1976?

> *Whom* is the direct object of the verb *did nominate.* This becomes clear if you restructure the question: *The Democratic Party did nominate whom in 1976?*

ON THE WEB   dianahacker.com/pocket

► **Language Debates**
  ► *who* versus *whom*

ON THE WEB dianahacker.com/pocket

▶ **Electronic grammar exercises**
  ▶ Grammar
    ▶ *who* and *whom*

---

13 Choose adjectives and adverbs with care.

Adjectives modify nouns or pronouns; adverbs modify verbs, adjectives, or other adverbs.

Many adverbs are formed by adding *-ly* to adjectives (*formal, formally*). But don't assume that all words ending in *-ly* are adverbs or that all adverbs end in *-ly*. Some adjectives end in *-ly* (*lovely, friendly*) and some adverbs don't (*always, here*). When in doubt, consult a dictionary.

13a Adverbs

Use adverbs, not adjectives, to modify verbs, adjectives, and adverbs. Adverbs usually answer one of these questions: When? Where? How? Why? Under what conditions? How often? To what degree?

The incorrect use of adjectives in place of adverbs to modify verbs occurs primarily in casual or nonstandard speech.

▶ The manager must see that the office runs
  ~~smooth~~ and ~~efficient.~~
    smoothly *efficiently.*

The incorrect use of the adjective *good* in place of the adverb *well* is especially common in casual and nonstandard speech.

▶ We were delighted that Nomo had done so ~~good~~
                                              well
  on the exam.

Adjectives are sometimes incorrectly used to modify adjectives or other adverbs.

▶ In the early 1970s, chances for survival of the bald
  eagle looked ~~real~~ slim.
               really

13b Adjectives

Adjectives ordinarily precede nouns, but they can also function as subject complements following linking verbs (usually a form of *be: be, am, is, are, was, were, being, been*). When an adjective functions as a subject complement, it describes the subject.

Justice is *blind*.

Problems can arise with verbs such as *smell, taste, look, appear, grow,* and *feel,* which may or may not be linking. If the word following one of these verbs describes the subject, use an adjective; if the word modifies the verb, use an adverb.

ADJECTIVE The detective looked *cautious.*

ADVERB The detective looked *cautiously* for the fingerprints.

Linking verbs usually suggest states of being, not actions. For example, to look cautious suggests the state of being cautious, whereas to look cautiously is to perform an action in a cautious way.

▶ Lori looked ~~well~~ *good* in her new raincoat.

▶ All of us on the debate team felt ~~badly~~ *bad* about our performance.

The verbs *looked* and *felt* suggest states of being, not actions, so they should be followed by adjectives.

ON THE WEB	dianahacker.com/pocket

▶ **Language Debates**
  ▶ *bad* versus *badly*

13c Comparatives and superlatives

Most adjectives and adverbs have three forms: the positive, the comparative, and the superlative.

POSITIVE	COMPARATIVE	SUPERLATIVE
soft	softer	softest
fast	faster	fastest
careful	more careful	most careful
bad	worse	worst
good	better	best

Comparative vs. superlative. Use the comparative to compare two things, the superlative to compare three or more.

▶ Which of these two brands of toothpaste is ~~best?~~ *better?*

▶ Hermos is the ~~more~~ *most* qualified of the three applicants.

Form of comparatives and superlatives To form comparatives and superlatives of most one- and two-syllable adjectives, use the endings -er and -est: *smooth, smoother, smoothest.* With longer adjectives, use *more* and *most* (or *less* and *least*): *exciting, more exciting, most exciting.*

Some one-syllable adverbs take the endings -er and -est (*fast, faster, fastest*), but longer adverbs and all of those ending in -ly use *more* and *most* (or *less* and *least*).

Double comparatives or superlatives. Do not use a double comparative (an -er ending and the word *more*) or a double superlative (an -est ending and the word *most*).

▶ All the polls indicated that Dewey was more ~~likelier~~ *likely* to win than Truman.

Absolute concepts. Do not use comparatives or superlatives with absolute concepts such as *unique* or *perfect.* Either something is unique or it isn't. It is illogical to suggest that absolute concepts come in degrees.

▶ That is the most ~~unique~~ *unusual* wedding gown I have ever seen.

14   Repair sentence fragments.

As a rule, do not treat a piece of a sentence as if it were a sentence. To be a sentence, a word group must consist of at least one full independent clause. An independent clause has a subject and a verb, and it either stands alone as a sentence or could stand alone. Some fragments are clauses that contain a subject and a verb but begin with a subordinating word. Others are phrases that lack a subject, a verb, or both.

You can repair a fragment in one of two ways: Either pull the fragment into a nearby sentence, punctuating the new sentence correctly, or turn the fragment into a sentence.

14a Fragmented clauses

A subordinate clause is patterned like a sentence, with both a subject and a verb, but it begins with a word that tells readers it cannot stand alone—a word such as *after, although, because, before, if, so that, that, though, unless, until, when, where, who,* or *which.*

Most fragmented clauses beg to be pulled into a sentence nearby.

▶ Patricia arrived on the island of Malta/, ~~Where~~ *where*

she was to spend the summer restoring frescoes.

If a fragmented clause cannot be gracefully combined with a nearby sentence, try rewriting it. The simplest way to turn a fragmented clause into a sentence is to delete the opening word or words that mark it as subordinate.

▶ Uncontrolled development is taking a deadly

toll on the environment. ~~So that in~~ *In* many parts

of the world, fragile ecosystems are collapsing.

14b Fragmented phrases

Like subordinate clauses, certain phrases are sometimes mistaken for sentences. Frequently a fragmented phrase may simply be attached to a nearby sentence.

▶ The archaeologists worked slowly/, ~~Examining~~ *examining* and

labeling every pottery shard they uncovered.

The word group beginning with *Examining* is a verbal phrase, not a sentence.

▶ Many adults suffer silently from agoraphobia/, ~~A~~ *a*

fear of the outside world.

A fear of the outside world is an appositive phrase, not a sentence.

▶ It has been said that there are only three

indigenous American art forms/: ~~Jazz,~~ *jazz,* musical

comedy, and soap operas.

Clearly the list is not a sentence. Notice how easily a colon corrects the problem. (See p. 75.)

If the fragmented phrase cannot be attached to a nearby sentence, turn the phrase into a sentence. You may need to add a subject, a verb, or both.

▶ If Eric doesn't get his way, he goes into a fit of rage.

               he lies

  For example, ~~lying~~ on the floor screaming or

 opens   _slams_

 ~~opening~~ the cabinet doors and then ~~slamming~~

 ^   ^

  them shut.

The writer corrected this fragment by adding a subject—
_he_—and substituting verbs for the verbals _lying, opening,_
and _slamming._

14c Acceptable fragments

Skilled writers occasionally use sentence fragments for
emphasis. In the following passage, Richard Rodriguez
uses a fragment (italicized) to draw attention to his
mother.

Following the dramatic Americanization of their
children, even my parents grew more publicly confi-
dent. _Especially my mother._ She learned the names of
all the people on our block.

                           —_Hunger of Memory_

  Although fragments are sometimes appropriate,
writers and readers do not always agree on when they
are appropriate. Therefore, you will find it safer to write
in complete sentences.

ON THE WEB   dianahacker.com/pocket

▶ **Electronic grammar exercises**
  ▶ **Grammar**
    ▶ Sentence fragments

---

15   Revise run-on sentences.

Run-on sentences are independent clauses that have
not been joined correctly. An independent clause is a
word group that does or could stand alone as a sentence. When two or more independent clauses appear
in one sentence, they must be joined in one of these
ways:

—with a comma and a coordinating conjunction (*and, but, or, nor, for, so, yet*)

—with a semicolon (or occasionally a colon or a dash)

There are two types of run-on sentences. When a writer puts no mark of punctuation and no coordinating conjunction between independent clauses, the result is a fused sentence.

FUSED Gestures are a means of communication for everyone they are essential for the hearing-impaired.

A far more common type of run-on sentence is the comma splice—two or more independent clauses joined by a comma without a coordinating conjunction. In some comma splices, the comma appears alone.

COMMA SPLICE Gestures are a means of communication for everyone, they are essential for the hearing-impaired.

In other comma splices, the comma is accompanied by a joining word that is *not* a coordinating conjunction. There are only seven coordinating conjunctions in English: *and, but, or, nor, for, so, yet*.

COMMA SPLICE Gestures are a means of communication for everyone, however, they are essential for the hearing-impaired.

The word *however* is a conjunctive adverb, not a coordinating conjunction. When a conjunctive adverb joins independent clauses, the clauses must be separated with a semicolon.

To correct a run-on sentence, you have four choices:

1. Use a comma and a coordinating conjunction.
2. Use a semicolon (or, if appropriate, a colon or a dash).
3. Make the clauses into separate sentences.
4. Restructure the sentence, perhaps by subordinating one of the clauses.

One of these revision techniques will usually work better than the others for a particular sentence. The fourth technique, the one requiring the most extensive revision, is frequently the most effective.

▶ Gestures are a means of communication for
         but
everyone, they are essential for the hearing-
              ^
impaired.

▶ Gestures are a means of communication for
         ;
everyone/they are essential for the hearing-
            ^
impaired.

▶ Gestures are a means of communication for
         T
everyone/. they are essential for the hearing-
             ^
impaired.

   Although gestures
▶ ~~Gestures~~ are a means of communication for
  ^
everyone, they are essential for the hearing-

impaired.

15a Revision with a comma and a coordinating conjunction

When a coordinating conjunction (*and, but, or, nor, for, so, yet*) joins independent clauses, it is usually preceded by a comma.

▶ Most of his contemporaries had made plans for
              but
their retirement, Tom had not.
                 ^

15b Revision with a semicolon (or a colon or a dash)

When the independent clauses are closely related and their relation is clear without a coordinating conjunction, a semicolon is an acceptable method of revision.

▶ Tragedy depicts the individual confronted with the
                ;
fact of death/comedy depicts the adaptability and
             ^
ongoing survival of human society.

A semicolon is required between independent clauses that have been linked with a conjunctive adverb such as *however* or *therefore* or a transitional phrase such as *in fact* or *of course*. (See p. 73 for a more complete list.)

▶ The timber wolf looks like a large German

shepherd/; however, the wolf has longer legs,
      ^

larger feet, and a wider head.

If the first independent clause introduces a quoted sentence, use a colon.

▶ Carolyn Heilbrun says this about the future/:
                                     ^

"Today's shocks are tomorrow's conventions."

Either a colon or a dash may be appropriate when the second clause summarizes or explains the first. (See also 18b and 21d.)

                                 : This
▶ Nuclear waste is hazardous ~~this~~ is an
                                      ^

indisputable fact.

▶ The female black widow spider is often a widow
                                   --
of her own making/ she has been known to eat
                     ^

her partner after mating.

15c Revision by separating sentences

If both independent clauses are long—or if one is a question and the other is not—consider making them separate sentences.

▶ Why should we spend money on expensive space
                  ? We
exploration/ ~~we~~ have enough underfunded
      ^

programs here on earth.

NOTE: When two quoted independent clauses are divided by explanatory words, make each clause its own sentence.

▶ "It's always smart to learn from your mistakes,"
                    "It's
quipped my boss/. "~~it's~~ even smarter to learn from
             ^

the mistakes of others."

15d Revision by restructuring the sentence

For sentence variety, consider restructuring the sentence, perhaps by turning one of the independent
clauses into a subordinate clause or phrase.

   Although many
▶ ~~Many~~ scholars dismiss the abominable snowman
  ^

of the Himalayas as a myth, others claim it may be

a kind of ape.

▶ Of the many geysers in Yellowstone National Park,
                            which
the most famous is Old Faithful, ~~it~~ sometimes
                         ^

reaches 150 feet in height.

▶ Mary McLeod Bethune,~~was~~ the seventeenth
                 ^

child of former slaves, ~~she~~ founded the National

Council of Negro Women in 1935.

ON THE WEB	dianahacker.com/pocket

▶ **Language Debates**
    ▶ Comma splices

ON THE WEB	dianahacker.com/pocket

▶ **Electronic grammar exercises**
    ▶ Grammar
        ▶ Run-ons

16 If English is not your native language, check for common ESL problems.

This section of *A Pocket Style Manual* has a special audience: speakers of English as a second language (ESL) who have learned English but continue to have difficulty with a few troublesome features of the language.

ON THE WEB ▶ dianahacker.com/pocket

▶ **Electronic grammar exercises**
  ▶ Grammar
    ▶ Articles
    ▶ Helping verbs and main verbs
    ▶ Omissions and repetitions

16a Articles

The definite article *the* and the indefinite articles *a* and *an* signal that a noun is about to appear. The noun may follow the article immediately or modifiers may intervene.

> *the cat, the* black *cat*
> *a sunset, a* spectacular *sunset*
> *an apple, an* appetizing *apple*

When to use a *(or* an*).*   Use *a* (or *an*) with singular count nouns whose specific identity is not known to the reader. Count nouns refer to persons, places, or things that can be counted: *one girl, two girls; one city, three cities.*

▶ Mary Beth arrived in ^*a* limousine.

▶ The biology student looked for ^*an* insect like the one

 in his textbook.

A (or *an*) usually means "one among many" but can also mean "any one."

NOTE: *A* is used before a consonant sound: *a banana, a happy child. An* is used before a vowel sound: *an eggplant, an honorable person.* See the Glossary of Usage.

When not to use a (*or* an).   *A* (or *an*) is not used to mark noncount nouns. Noncount nouns refer to entities or abstractions that cannot be counted: *water, silver, sugar, furniture, patience.* (See below for a fuller list.)

▶ Claudia asked her mother for ~~an~~ advice.

If you want to express an amount of something designated by a noncount noun, you can often add a quantifier in front of it: *a quart of milk, an ounce of gold, a piece of furniture.*

NOTE: A few noncount nouns may also be used as count nouns: *Bill loves coffee; Bill offered me a coffee.*

COMMONLY USED NONCOUNT NOUNS

Food and drink: bacon, beef, bread, broccoli, butter, cabbage, candy, cauliflower, celery, cereal, cheese, chicken, chocolate, coffee, corn, cream, fish, flour, fruit, ice cream, lettuce, meat, milk, oil, pasta, rice, salt, spinach, sugar, tea, water, wine, yogurt

Nonfood substances: air, cement, coal, dirt, gasoline, gold, paper, petroleum, plastic, rain, silver, snow, soap, steel, wood, wool

Abstract nouns: advice, anger, beauty, confidence, courage, employment, fun, happiness, health, honesty, information, intelligence, knowledge, love, poverty, satisfaction, truth, wealth

Other: biology (and other areas of study), clothing, equipment, furniture, homework, jewelry, luggage, lumber, machinery, mail, money, news, poetry, pollution, research, scenery, traffic, transportation, violence, weather, work

---

When to use the.   Use the definite article *the* with most nouns whose specific identity is known to the reader. Usually the identity will be clear for one of these reasons:

1. The noun has been previously mentioned.
2. A word group following the noun restricts its identity.
3. The context or situation makes the noun's identity clear.

▶ A truck loaded with manure cut in front of our

       the

van. When truck skidded a few seconds later, we

    ^

almost plowed into it.

The noun *truck* is preceded by *A* when it is first mentioned. When the noun is mentioned again, it is preceded by *the* since readers now know the specific truck being discussed.

           the

▶ Bob warned me that printer in the shipping

          ^

department was broken.

The phrase *in the shipping department* identifies the specific printer.

      the

▶ Please don't slam door when you leave.

       ^

Both the speaker and the listener know which door is meant.

When not to use **the.** Do not use *the* with plural or non-count nouns meaning "all" or "in general."

  F

▶ ~~The~~ ƒountains are an expensive element of

landscape design.

▶ In some parts of the world, ~~the~~ rice is preferred to

all other grains.

Although there are many exceptions, do not use *the* with most singular proper nouns: names of persons (Jessica Webner); names of streets, squares, parks, cities, and states (Prospect Street, Union Square, Denali National Park, Miami, Idaho); names of continents and most countries (South America, Italy); and names of bays and single lakes, mountains, and islands (Tampa Bay, Lake Geneva, Mount Everest, Crete).

Exceptions to this rule include names of large regions, deserts, and peninsulas (the East Coast, the Sahara, the Iberian Peninsula) and names of oceans, seas, gulfs, canals, and rivers (the Pacific, the Dead Sea, the Persian Gulf, the Panama Canal, the Amazon).

NOTE: *The* is used to mark plural proper nouns: the United Nations, the Finger Lakes, the Andes, the Bahamas.

16b Helping verbs and main verbs

Only certain combinations of helping verbs and main verbs make sense in English. The correct combinations are discussed in this section, after the following review of helping verbs and main verbs.

Review. Helping verbs always appear before main verbs.

> HV MV   HV   MV
> We *will leave* at noon. *Do* you *want* a ride?

Some helping verbs—*have, do,* and *be*—change form to indicate tenses; others, known as modals, do not.

FORMS OF *HAVE, DO,* AND *BE*

have, has, had
do, does, did
be, am, is, are, was, were, being, been

MODALS

can, could, may, might, must, shall, should, will, would
(*also* ought to)

Every main verb has five forms (except *be,* which has eight). The following list shows these forms for the regular verb *help* and the irregular verb *give.* (See pp. 30–32 for a list of common irregular verbs.)

BASE FORM	help, give
–S FORM	helps, gives
PAST TENSE	helped, gave
PAST PARTICIPLE	helped, given
PRESENT PARTICIPLE	helping, giving

Modal + base form. After the modals *can, could, may, might, must, shall, should, will,* and *would,* use the base form of the verb.

▶ Geologists predicted that a minor earthquake

would occur~~s~~ along the Santa Ana fault line.

speak
► We could ~~spoke~~ Spanish when we were young.
            ^

Do, does, *or* **did** + *base form.*   After helping verbs that are a form of *do,* use the base form of the verb.

► Mariko does not want~~s~~ any more dessert.

buy
► Did Janice ~~bought~~ the gift for Katherine?
             ^

Have, has, *or* **had** + *past participle.*   To form one of the perfect tenses, use *have, has,* or *had* followed by a past participle (usually ending in *-ed, -d, -en, -n,* or *-t*). (See perfect tenses, pp. 33–34.)

                    offered
► Many churches have ~~offer~~ shelter to the homeless.
                      ^

               spoken
► An-Mei has not ~~speaking~~ Chinese since she was a
                  ^

child.

Form of **be** + *present participle.*   To express an action in progress, use *am, is, are, was, were, be,* or *been* followed by a present participle (the *-ing* form of the verb).

                            turning
► Because it is a clear night, I am ~~turn~~ my
                                     ^

telescope to the constellation Cassiopeia.

           driving
► Uncle Roy was ~~driven~~ a brand-new red
                 ^

Corvette.

The helping verbs *be* and *been* must be preceded by other helping verbs. See the progressive forms listed on page 34.

CAUTION: Certain verbs are not normally used in the progressive sense in English. In general, these verbs express a state of being or mental activity, not a dynamic action. Common examples are *appear, believe, have, hear, know, like, need, see, seem, taste, think, understand,* and *want.*

want
▶ I ~~am wanting~~ to see August Wilson's *Seven Guitars*
  ^

at Arena Stage.

Form of be + *past participle.*   To form the passive voice,
use *am, are, was, were, being, be,* or *been* followed by a
past participle (usually ending in *-ed, -d, -en, -n,* or *-t*).
When a sentence is written in the passive voice, the
subject of the sentence receives the action instead of
doing it. (See pp. 3–5.)

    written
▶ *Bleak House* was ~~write~~ by Charles Dickens.
      ^
      honored
▶ The scientists were ~~honor~~ for their work with
       ^

endangered species.

In the passive voice, the helping verb *be* must be
preceded by a modal: *Senator Dixon will be defeated. Being* must be preceded by *am, is, are, was,* or *were: The
child was being teased. Been* must be preceded by *have,
has,* or *had: I have been invited to a party.*

CAUTION: Although they may seem to have passive meanings, verbs such as *occur, happen, sleep, die,* and *fall* may
not be used to form the passive voice because they are
intransitive. Only transitive verbs, those that take direct
objects, may be used to form the passive voice.

▶ The earthquake ~~was~~ occurred last Friday.

16c Omitted subjects, expletives, or verbs

Some languages allow omission of subjects, expletives,
or verbs in certain contexts. English does not.

English requires a subject for all sentences except
imperatives, in which the subject *you* is understood
(*Give to the poor*). If your native language allows the
omission of an explicit subject, be especially alert to this
requirement in English.

 I have
▶ ~~Have~~ a large collection of baseball cards.
  ^

he
► My brother is very bright; could read a book
^

before he started school.

When the subject has been moved from its normal position before the verb, English sometimes requires an expletive (*there* or *it*) at the beginning of the sentence or clause.

there
► As you know, are many religious sects in India.
^

It is
► ~~Is~~ healthy to eat fruit and grains.
^

The subjects of these sentences are *sects* and *to eat fruit and grains*.

Although some languages allow the omission of the verb when the meaning is clear without it, English does not.

is
► Powell Street in San Francisco very steep.
^

16d Repeated subjects or objects

English does not allow a subject to be repeated in its own clause. This is true even if a word group intervenes between the subject and the verb.

► The painting that had been stolen ~~it~~ was found.

The pronoun *it* repeats the subject *painting*.

In some languages an object is repeated later in the adjective clause in which it appears; in English, such repetitions are not allowed. Adjective clauses usually begin with *who, whom, whose, which,* or *that,* and these relative pronouns always serve a grammatical function within the clauses they introduce. Another word in the clause cannot also serve that same function.

► The puppy ran after the taxi that we were riding

in. ~~it.~~
^

The relative pronoun *that* is the object of the preposition *in,* so the object *it* is not allowed.

Even when the relative pronoun has been omitted, do not add another word with its same function.

▶ The puppy ran after the taxi we were riding in. ~~it.~~
                                                    ^

The relative pronoun *that* is understood.

The comma was invented to help readers. Without it, sentence parts can collide into one another unexpectedly, causing misreadings.

CONFUSING   If you cook Elmer will do the dishes.

CONFUSING   While we were eating a rattlesnake
                     approached our campsite.

Add commas in the logical places (after *cook* and *eating*), and suddenly all is clear. No longer is Elmer being cooked, the rattlesnake being eaten.

     Various rules have evolved to prevent such misreadings and to guide readers through complex grammatical structures. According to most experts, you should use a comma in the following situations.

17a   Before a coordinating conjunction joining independent clauses

When a coordinating conjunction connects two or more independent clauses—word groups that could stand alone as separate sentences—a comma must precede it. There are seven coordinating conjunctions in English: *and, but, or, nor, for, so,* and *yet.*

     A comma tells readers that one independent clause has come to a close and that another is about to begin.

> ▶   Nearly everyone has heard of love at first sight,
>
>   ^
>
>   but I fell in love at first dance.

EXCEPTION: If the two independent clauses are short and there is no danger of misreading, the comma may be omitted.

     The plane took off and we were on our way.

CAUTION: Do *not* use a comma to separate compound elements that are not independent clauses. See page 71.

17b   After an introductory word group

Use a comma after an introductory clause or phrase. A comma tells readers that the introductory word group has come to a close and that the main part of the sentence is about to begin. The most common introductory word groups are adverb clauses, prepositional phrases, and participial phrases.

▶ When Strom Thurmond ran for president in 1948, he was a staunch segregationist.

▶ Near a small stream at the bottom of the canyon, we discovered an abandoned shelter.

▶ Buried under layers of younger rocks, the earth's oldest rocks contain no fossils.

EXCEPTION: The comma may be omitted after a short clause or phrase if there is no danger of misreading.

In no time we were at 2,800 feet.

17c Between items in a series

Use a comma between all items in a series, including the last two.

▶ Bubbles of air, leaves, ferns, bits of wood, and insects are often found trapped in amber.

Although some writers view the comma between the last two items as optional, most experts advise using it because its omission can result in ambiguity or misreading.

ON THE WEB   dianahacker.com/pocket

▶ **Language Debates**
   ▶ Commas with items in a series

17d Between coordinate adjectives

Use a comma between coordinate adjectives, those that each modify a noun separately.

▶ Patients with severe, irreversible brain damage
   ^

should not be put on life support systems.

Adjectives are coordinate if they can be connected with *and: severe and irreversible.*

CAUTION: Do not use a comma between cumulative adjectives, those that do not each modify the noun separately.

Three large gray shapes moved slowly toward us.

Adjectives are cumulative if they cannot be connected with *and.* It would be very odd to say *three and large and gray shapes.*

17e To set off a nonrestrictive element

A *restrictive* element restricts the meaning of the word it modifies and is therefore essential to the meaning of the sentence. It is not set off with commas. A *nonrestrictive* element describes a word whose meaning already is clear. It is not essential to the meaning of the sentence and is set off with commas.

RESTRICTIVE

For camp the children needed clothes *that were washable.*

NONRESTRICTIVE

For camp the children needed sturdy shoes, *which were expensive.*

If you remove a restrictive element from a sentence, the meaning changes significantly, becoming more general than intended. The writer of the first sample sentence does not mean that the children needed clothes in general. The meaning is more restricted: The children needed *washable* clothes.

If you remove a nonrestrictive element from a sentence, the meaning does not change significantly. Some meaning is lost, to be sure, but the defining characteristics of the person or thing described remain the same as before. The children needed *sturdy shoes,* and these happened to be expensive.

Elements that may be restrictive or nonrestrictive include adjective clauses, adjective phrases, and appositives.

Adjective clauses. Adjective clauses, which usually follow the noun or pronoun they describe, begin with a relative pronoun (*who, whom, whose, which, that*) or a relative adverb (*when, where*). When an adjective clause is nonrestrictive, set it off with commas; when it is restrictive, omit the commas.

NONRESTRICTIVE CLAUSE

▶ A 1911 fire at the Triangle Shirtwaist Company,
  which killed 146 sweatshop workers, led to reforms
  in working conditions.

RESTRICTIVE CLAUSE

▶ A corporation/ that has government contracts/ must
  maintain careful personnel records.

NOTE: Use *that* only with restrictive clauses. Many writers use *which* only with nonrestrictive clauses, but usage varies.

ON THE WEB dianahacker.com/pocket

▶ **Language Debates**
  ▶ *that* versus *which*

Adjective phrases. Prepositional or verbal phrases functioning as adjectives may be restrictive or nonrestrictive. Nonrestrictive phrases are set off with commas; restrictive phrases are not.

NONRESTRICTIVE PHRASE

▶ The helicopter, with its 100,000-candlepower
  spotlight illuminating the area, circled above.

RESTRICTIVE PHRASE

▶ One corner of the attic was filled with newspapers/

dating from the turn of the 1920s.

Appositives.   An appositive is a noun or pronoun that re-names a nearby noun. Nonrestrictive appositives are set off with commas; restrictive appositives are not.

NONRESTRICTIVE APPOSITIVE

▶ Darwin's most important book‸ *On the Origin of*

Species‸ was the result of many years of research.

RESTRICTIVE APPOSITIVE

▶ The song/ "Fire It Up/" was blasted out of

amplifiers ten feet tall.

17f   To set off transitional and parenthetical expressions, absolute phrases, and contrasted elements

Transitional expressions.   Transitional expressions serve as bridges between sentences or parts of sentences. They include conjunctive adverbs such as *however, therefore,* and *moreover* and transitional phrases such as *for example* and *as a matter of fact.* For a more com-plete list, see page 73.

When a transitional expression appears between independent clauses in a compound sentence, it is pre-ceded by a semicolon and usually followed by a comma.

▶ Minh did not understand our language; moreover‸

he was unfamiliar with our customs.

When a transitional expression appears at the be-ginning of a sentence or in the middle of an indepen-dent clause, it is usually set off with commas.

▶ As a matter of fact, American football was established by fans who wanted to play a more organized game of rugby.

▶ Natural foods are not always salt free; celery, for example, contains more sodium than most people would imagine.

Parenthetical expressions. Expressions that are distinctly parenthetical, interrupting the flow of a sentence, should be set off with commas.

▶ Evolution, so far as we know, does not work this way.

Absolute phrases. An absolute phrase, which modifies the whole sentence, should be set off with commas.

▶ Our grant having been approved, we were at last able to begin the archaeological dig.

Contrasted elements. Sharp contrasts beginning with words such as *not* and *unlike* are set off with commas.

▶ The Epicurean philosophers sought mental, not bodily, pleasures.

17g To set off nouns of direct address, the words *yes* and *no*, interrogative tags, and mild interjections

▶ Forgive us, Dr. Spock, for spanking Brian.

▶ Yes, the loan will probably be approved.

▶ The film was faithful to the book, wasn't it?

▶ Well, cases like this are difficult to decide.

17h To set off direct quotations introduced with expressions such as *he said*

▶ Naturalist Arthur Cleveland Bent remarked, "In part the peregrine declined unnoticed because it is not adorable."

17i With dates, addresses, titles

Dates. In dates, the year is set off from the rest of the sentence with commas.

▶ On December 12, 1890, orders were sent out for the arrest of Sitting Bull.

EXCEPTIONS: Commas are not needed if the date is inverted or if only the month and year are given: *The deadline is 15 April 2004. May 2003 was a surprisingly cold month.*

Addresses. The elements of an address or place name are followed by commas. A zip code, however, is not preceded by a comma.

▶ Greg lived at 708 Spring Street, Washington, Illinois 61571.

Titles. If a title follows a name, separate it from the rest of the sentence with a pair of commas.

▶ Sandra Barnes, M.D., performed the surgery.

17j Misuses of the comma

Do not use commas unless you have a good reason for using them. In particular, avoid using the comma in the following situations.

BETWEEN COMPOUND ELEMENTS THAT ARE NOT INDEPENDENT CLAUSES

▶ Marie Curie discovered radium,/and later applied her work on radioactivity to medicine.

TO SEPARATE A VERB FROM ITS SUBJECT

▶ Zoos large enough to give the animals freedom to roam,/are becoming more popular.

BETWEEN CUMULATIVE ADJECTIVES (See p. 66.)

▶ Joyce was wearing a slinky,/red silk gown.

TO SET OFF RESTRICTIVE ELEMENTS (See pp. 66–68.)

▶ Drivers,/who think they own the road,/make cycling a dangerous sport.

▶ Margaret Mead's book/ *Coming of Age in Samoa*/ caused controversy when it was published.

AFTER A COORDINATING CONJUNCTION

▶ Occasionally soap operas are live, but,/more often they are taped.

AFTER *SUCH AS* OR *LIKE*

▶ Plants such as,/begonias and impatiens add color to a shady garden.

BEFORE *THAN*

▶ Touring Crete was more thrilling for us,/than visiting the Greek islands frequented by the jet set.

BEFORE A PARENTHESIS

► At MCI Sylvia began at the bottom⁄(with only a
cubicle and a swivel chair), but within five years
she had been promoted to supervisor.

TO SET OFF AN INDIRECT (REPORTED) QUOTATION

► Samuel Goldwyn once said⁄that a verbal contract
isn't worth the paper it's written on.

WITH A QUESTION MARK OR AN EXCLAMATION POINT

► "Why don't you try it?⁄" she coaxed.

ON THE WEB   dianahacker.com/pocket

► **Electronic grammar exercises**
    ► Punctuation
        ► Commas

---

18 The semicolon and the colon

18a The semicolon

The semicolon is used between independent clauses
not joined by a coordinating conjunction. It can also be
used between items in a series containing internal
punctuation.

The semicolon is never used between elements of
unequal grammatical rank.

Between independent clauses.   When related independent
clauses appear in one sentence, they are ordinarily connected with a comma and a coordinating conjunction
(*and, but, or, nor, for, so, yet*). The coordinating conjunction expresses the relation between the clauses. If the
relation is clear without a conjunction, a writer may
choose to connect the clauses with a semicolon instead.

Injustice is relatively easy to bear; what stings is
justice.   —H. L. Mencken

A writer may also choose to connect the clauses
with a semicolon and a conjunctive adverb such as
however or *therefore* or a transitional phrase such as *for
example* or *in fact*.

He swallowed a lot of wisdom; however, it seemed as
if all of it had gone down the wrong way.
                                            —G. C. Lichtenberg

CONJUNCTIVE ADVERBS	accordingly, also, anyway, besides, certainly, consequently, conversely, finally, furthermore, hence, however, incidentally, indeed, instead, likewise, meanwhile, moreover, nevertheless, next, nonetheless, otherwise, similarly, specifically, still, subsequently, then, therefore, thus
TRANSITIONAL PHRASES	after all, as a matter of fact, as a result, at any rate, at the same time, even so, for example, for instance, in addition, in conclusion, in fact, in other words, in the first place, on the contrary, on the other hand

CAUTION: A semicolon must be used whenever a coordinating conjunction has been omitted between independent clauses. To use merely a comma—or to use a comma and a conjunctive adverb or transitional expression—creates an error known as a comma splice. (See p. 51.)

▶ In 1800, a traveler needed six weeks to get from
   New York City to Chicago; in 1860, the trip by
   railroad took only two days.

▶ Many corals grow very gradually; in fact, the
   creation of a coral reef can take centuries.

Between items in a series containing internal punctuation.
Ordinarily, items in a series are separated by commas.
If one or more of the items contain internal punctuation, however, a writer may use semicolons instead.

Classic science fiction sagas are *Star Trek,* with Mr. Spock and his large pointed ears; *Battlestar Galactica,* with its Cylon raiders; and *Star Wars,* with Han Solo, Luke Skywalker, and Darth Vader.

Misuses of the semicolon. Do not use a semicolon in the following situations.

BETWEEN AN INDEPENDENT AND A SUBORDINATE CLAUSE

▶ The media like to portray my generation as lazy**;** although polls show that we work as hard as the twentysomethings before us.

BETWEEN AN APPOSITIVE AND THE WORD IT REFERS TO

▶ We were fascinated by the species *Argyroneta aquatica***;** a spider that lives underwater.

TO INTRODUCE A LIST

▶ Some of my favorite film stars have home pages on the Web**;** John Travolta, Susan Sarandon, Brad Pitt, and Emma Thompson.

BETWEEN INDEPENDENT CLAUSES JOINED BY *AND, BUT, OR, NOR, FOR, SO,* **OR** *YET*

▶ Five of the applicants had worked with spread-sheets**;** but only one was familiar with database management.

18b The colon

The colon is used after an independent clause to call attention to the words that follow it. The colon also has certain conventional uses.

Main uses of the colon. After an independent clause, a writer may use a colon to direct the reader's attention to a list, an appositive, or a quotation.

A LIST

> The routine includes the following: twenty knee bends, fifty leg lifts, and five minutes of running in place.

AN APPOSITIVE

> My roommate is guilty of two of the seven deadly sins: gluttony and sloth.

A QUOTATION

> Consider the words of John F. Kennedy: "Ask not what your country can do for you; ask what you can do for your country."

For other ways of introducing quotations, see pages 81–82.

A colon may also be used between independent clauses if the second summarizes or explains the first.

> Faith is like love. It cannot be forced.

The second clause may begin with a capital or a lowercase letter.

> Minds are like parachutes: They [*or* they] function only when open.

Other uses. Use a colon after the salutation in a formal letter, to indicate hours and minutes, to show proportions, between a title and subtitle, and to separate city and publisher in bibliographic entries.

> Dear Sir or Madam:
>
> 5:30 P.M. (or p.m.)
>
> The ratio of women to men was 2:1.
>
> *Alvin Ailey: A Life in Dance*
>
> Boston: Bedford, 2004

NOTE: In biblical references, a colon is ordinarily used between chapter and verse (Luke 2:14). The Modern Language Association recommends a period (Luke 2.14).

Misuses of the colon. A colon must be preceded by an independent clause. Therefore, avoid using it in the following situations.

BETWEEN A VERB AND ITS OBJECT OR COMPLEMENT

▶ Some important vitamins found in vegetables are⫶

vitamin A, thiamine, niacin, and vitamin C.

BETWEEN A PREPOSITION AND ITS OBJECT

▶ The heart's two pumps each consist of⫶ an upper

chamber, or atrium, and a lower chamber, or

ventricle.

AFTER *SUCH AS, INCLUDING,* OR *FOR EXAMPLE*

▶ The trees on campus include fine Japanese

specimens such as⫶ black pines, ginkgos, and

cutleaf maples.

ON THE WEB dianahacker.com/pocket
▶ **Electronic grammar exercises**
  ▶ Punctuation
    ▶ The semicolon and the colon

---

19 The apostrophe

The apostrophe is used to indicate possession and to mark contractions. In addition, it has a few conventional uses.

19a To indicate possession

The apostrophe is used to indicate that a noun is possessive. Possessive nouns usually indicate ownership, as in *Tim's hat* or *the editor's desk*. Frequently, however, ownership is only loosely implied: *the tree's roots, a day's work.* If you are not sure whether a noun is possessive, try turning it into an *of* phrase: *the roots of the tree, the work of a day.*

When to add -'s.   Add -'s if the noun does not end in -s or if the noun is singular and ends in -s.

> Luck often propels a rock musician's career.

> Thank you for refunding the children's money.

> Lois's sister spent last year in India.

EXCEPTION: If pronunciation would be awkward with the added -'s, some writers use only the apostrophe: *Sophocles' plays are among my favorites.* Either use is acceptable.

When to add only an apostrophe.   If the noun is plural and ends in -s, add only an apostrophe.

> Both diplomats' briefcases were stolen.

Joint possession.   To show joint possession, use -'s (or -s') with the last noun only; to show individual possession, make all nouns possessive.

> Have you seen Joyce and Greg's new camper?

> Hernando's and Maria's expectations were quite different.

Compound nouns.   If a noun is compound, use -'s (or -s') with the last element.

> Her father-in-law's sculpture won first place.

Indefinite pronouns such as someone.   Use -'s to indicate that an indefinite pronoun is possessive. Indefinite pronouns refer to no specific person or thing: *everyone, someone, no one,* and so on.

> This diet will improve almost anyone's health.

19b To mark contractions

In a contraction, an apostrophe takes the place of missing letters.

It's a shame that Frank can't go on the tour.

It's stands for *it is,* can't for *cannot.*

The apostrophe is also used to mark the omission of the first two digits of a year (*the class of '99*) or years (*the '60s generation*).

19c Conventional uses

Traditionally, an apostrophe has been used to pluralize numbers, letters, abbreviations, and words mentioned as words. The trend, however, is toward omitting the apostrophe. Either use is correct, but be consistent.

Plural numbers and abbreviations.   To pluralize a number or an abbreviation, you may add *-s* or *-'s.*

Peggy skated nearly perfect figure 8s (*or* 8's).

We collected only four IOUs (*or* IOU's) out of forty.

NOTE: To pluralize decades, most current writers omit the apostrophe: 1920s (*not* 1920's)

Plural letters.   Italicize the letter and use roman type for the *-s* ending. Use of an apostrophe is usually optional; the Modern Language Association continues to recommend the apostrophe.

Two large *J*s (or *J*'s) were painted on the door.

Plurals of words mentioned as words.   Italicize the word and use roman type for the *-s* ending. Use of an apostrophe is optional.

We've heard enough *maybe*s (or *maybe*'s).

Words mentioned as words may also appear in quotation marks. When you choose this option, use the apostrophe: We've heard enough "maybe's."

19d Misuses of the apostrophe

Do not use an apostrophe in the following situations.

WITH NOUNS THAT ARE NOT POSSESSIVE

> *outpatients*
> ► Some ~~outpatient's~~ are given special parking
>   ^

permits.

IN THE POSSESSIVE PRONOUNS *ITS, WHOSE, HIS, HERS, OURS, YOURS,*
AND *THEIRS*

> *its*
> ► Each area has ~~it's~~ own conference room.
>   ^

It's means *it is*. The possessive pronoun *its* contains no
apostrophe despite the fact that it is possessive.

ON THE WEB	dianahacker.com/pocket

► **Electronic grammar exercises**
  ► Punctuation
    ► The apostrophe

---

20 Quotation marks

Quotation marks are used to enclose direct quotations.
They are also used around some titles and to set off
words used as words.

20a To enclose direct quotations

Direct quotations of a person's words, whether spoken
or written, must be in quotation marks.

> "A foolish consistency is the hobgoblin of little
> minds," wrote Ralph Waldo Emerson.

EXCEPTION: When a long quotation has been set off from
the text by indenting, quotation marks are not needed.
(See pp. 122, 163, and 191.)

Use single quotation marks to enclose a quotation
within a quotation.

> According to Paul Eliott, Eskimo hunters "chant an
> ancient magic song to the seal they are after: 'Beast
> of the sea! Come and place yourself before me in the
> early morning!'"

20b Around titles of short works

Use quotation marks around titles of newspaper and magazine articles, poems, short stories, songs, episodes of television and radio programs, and chapters or subdivisions of books.

> The poem "Mother to Son" is by Langston Hughes.

NOTE: Titles of books, plays, and films and names of magazines and newspapers are put in italics or underlined. (See pp. 93–94.)

20c To set off words used as words

Although words used as words are ordinarily underlined or italicized (see pp. 94–95), quotation marks are also acceptable.

> The words "affect" and "effect" are frequently confused.

20d Other punctuation with quotation marks

This section describes the conventions to observe in placing various marks of punctuation inside or outside quotation marks. It also explains how to punctuate when introducing quoted material.

Periods and commas.   Place periods and commas inside quotation marks.

> "This is a stick-up," said the well-dressed young couple. "We want all your money."

This rule applies to single and double quotation marks, and it applies to all uses of quotation marks.

NOTE: MLA and APA parenthetical citations are an exception to this rule. Put the parenthetical citation after the quotation mark and before the period. MLA: *According to Cole, "The instruments of science have vastly extended our senses" (53).* APA: *According to Cole (1999), "The instruments of science have vastly extended our senses" (p. 53).*

Colons and semicolons.   Put colons and semicolons outside quotation marks.

Harold wrote, "I regret that I cannot attend the AIDS fundraiser"; his letter, however, contained a contribution.

Question marks and exclamation points. Put question marks and exclamation points inside quotation marks unless they apply to the sentence as a whole.

Contrary to tradition, bedtime at my house is marked by "Mommy, can I tell you a story now?"

Have you heard the old proverb "Do not climb the hill until you reach it"?

In the first sentence, the question mark applies only to the quoted question. In the second sentence, the question mark applies to the whole sentence.

Introducing quoted material. After a word group introducing a quotation, use a colon, a comma, or no punctuation at all, whichever is appropriate in context.

If a quotation has been formally introduced, a colon is appropriate. A formal introduction is a full independent clause, not just an expression such as *he said* or *she writes*.

Morrow views personal ads as an art form: "The personal ad is like a haiku of self-celebration, a brief solo played on one's own horn."

If a quotation is introduced or followed by an expression such as *he said* or *she writes,* use a comma.

Stephen Leacock once said, "I am a great believer in luck, and I find the harder I work the more I have of it."

"You can be a little ungrammatical if you come from the right part of the country," writes Robert Frost.

When you blend a quotation into your own sentence, use either a comma or no punctuation, depending on the way in which the quotation fits into the sentence structure.

The champion could, as he put it, "float like a butterfly and sting like a bee."

Hudson notes that the prisoners escaped "by squeezing through a tiny window eighteen feet above the floor of their cell."

If a quotation appears at the beginning of a sentence, set it off with a comma unless the quotation ends with a question mark or an exclamation point.

> "We shot them like dogs," boasted Davy Crockett, who was among Jackson's troops.

> "What is it?" I asked, bracing myself.

If a quoted sentence is interrupted by explanatory words, use commas to set off the explanatory words.

> "A great many people think they are thinking," observed William James, "when they are merely rearranging their prejudices."

If two successive quoted sentences from the same source are interrupted by explanatory words, use a comma before the explanatory words and a period after them.

> "I was a flop as a daily reporter," admitted E. B. White. "Every piece had to be a masterpiece—and before you knew it, Tuesday was Wednesday."

20e Misuses of quotation marks

Do not use quotation marks to draw attention to familiar slang, to disown trite expressions, or to justify an attempt at humor.

▶ Between Thanksgiving and Super Bowl Sunday,

many American wives become ⌜football widows.⌟

Do not use quotation marks around indirect quotations. Indirect quotations report a person's words instead of quoting them directly.

▶ After leaving the scene of the domestic quarrel,

the officer said that ⌜he was due for a coffee

break.⌟

Do not use quotation marks around the title of your own essay.

ON THE WEB ▶ dianahacker.com/pocket

▶ **Electronic grammar exercises**
   ▶ Punctuation
      ▶ Quotation marks

21   Other marks

21a   The period

Use a period to end all sentences except direct questions or genuine exclamations. Use a period, not a question mark, for an indirect question—that is, a reported question.

> Celia asked whether the picnic would be canceled.

A period is conventionally used with personal titles, Latin abbreviations, academic degrees, systems of chronology, and designations of time.

Mr.	i.e.	Ph.D.	B.C.	A.M. (or a.m.)
Ms.	e.g.	R.N.	B.C.E.	P.M. (or p.m.)
Dr.	etc.	B.A.	A.D.	
		LL.D.		

A period is not used with postal service abbreviations for states, organization names, and most capitalized abbreviations.

CA	TX	NATO	IRS
NY	USA	AFL-CIO	FCC

Usage varies, however. When in doubt, consult a dictionary, a style manual, or a publication by the agency in question. Even the yellow pages can help.

NOTE: If a sentence ends with a period marking an abbreviation, do not add a second period.

21b   The question mark

Use a question mark after a direct question.

> What is the horsepower of a 747 engine?

If a polite request is written in the form of a question, you may use a question mark, though usage varies.

> Would you please send me your catalog of lilies?

CAUTION: Use a period, not a question mark, after an indirect question, one that is reported rather than asked directly.

> He asked me who was teaching the mythology course.

21c The exclamation point

Use an exclamation point after a sentence that expresses exceptional feeling or deserves special emphasis.

> We yelled to the police officer, "He's not drunk! He's in diabetic shock!"

CAUTION: Do not overuse the exclamation point.

▶ In the fisherman's memory the fish lives on,

increasing in length and weight with each passing

year, until at last it is big enough to shade a

fishing boat.
   ^

This sentence doesn't need to be pumped up with an exclamation point. It is emphatic enough without it.

21d The dash

The dash may be used to set off material that deserves special emphasis. When typing, use two hyphens to form a dash (- -), with no spaces before or after them. (If your word processing program has what is known as an "em-dash," you may use it instead, with no space before or after it.)

Use a dash to introduce a list, a restatement, an amplification, or a dramatic shift in tone or thought.

> Along the wall are the bulk liquids—sesame seed oil, honey, safflower oil, and half-liquid peanut butter.

> Consider the amount of sugar in the average person's diet—104 pounds per year.

> Kiere took a few steps back, came running full speed, kicked a mighty kick—and missed the ball.

In the first two examples, the writer could also use a colon. (See 18b.) The colon is more formal than the dash and not quite as dramatic.

Use a pair of dashes to set off parenthetical material that deserves special emphasis or to set off an appositive that contains commas.

> Everything that went wrong—from the peeping Tom at her window to my head-on collision—was blamed on our move.

> In my hometown the basic needs of people—food, clothing, and shelter—are less costly than in Denver.

CAUTION: Unless you have a specific reason for using the dash, avoid it. Unnecessary dashes create a choppy effect.

21e Parentheses

Use parentheses to enclose supplemental material, minor digressions, and afterthoughts.

> After taking her temperature, pulse, and blood pressure (routine vital signs), the nurse made Becky comfortable.

Use parentheses to enclose letters or numbers labeling items in a series.

> There are three points of etiquette in poker:
> (1) always allow someone to cut the cards,
> (2) don't forget to ante up, and (3) never stack your chips.

CAUTION: Do not overuse parentheses. Often a sentence reads more gracefully without them.

> *from ten to fifty million*
> ▶ Researchers have said that ~~ten million (estimates~~
> ^
> ~~run as high as fifty million)~~ Americans have
> hypoglycemia.

21f Brackets

Use brackets to enclose any words or phrases inserted into an otherwise word-for-word quotation.

> *Audubon* reports that "if there are not enough young to balance deaths, the end of the species [California condor] is inevitable."

The *Audubon* article did not contain the words *California condor* in the sentence quoted.

The Latin word "sic" in brackets indicates that an error in a quoted sentence appears in the original source.

> According to the review, k.d. lang's performance was brilliant, "exceding [sic] the expectations of even her most loyal fans."

21g The ellipsis mark

Use an ellipsis mark, three spaced periods, to indicate that you have deleted material from an otherwise word-for-word quotation.

> Reuben reports that "when the amount of cholesterol circulating in the blood rises over . . . 300 milligrams per 100, the chances of a heart attack increase dramatically."

If you delete a full sentence or more in the middle of a quoted passage, use a period before the three ellipsis dots.

CAUTION: Do not use the ellipsis mark at the beginning of a quotation; do not use it at the end of a quotation unless you have cut some words from the end of the final sentence quoted.

21h The slash

Use the slash to separate two or three lines of poetry that have been run in with your text. Add a space both before and after the slash.

> In the opening lines of "Jordan," George Herbert pokes fun at popular poems of his time: "Who says that fictions only and false hair / Become a verse? Is there in truth no beauty?"

Use the slash sparingly, if at all, to separate options: *pass/fail, producer/director.* Put no space around the slash. Avoid using a slash for *he/she, and/or,* and *his/her.*

ON THE WEB   dianahacker.com/pocket

▶ **Electronic grammar exercises**
   ▶ Punctuation
      ▶ Other punctuation marks

Mechanics

22 Capitalization

In addition to the following guidelines, a good dictionary can often tell you when to use capital letters.

22a Proper vs. common nouns

Proper nouns and words derived from them are capitalized; common nouns are not. Proper nouns name specific persons, places, and things. All other nouns are common nouns.

The following types of words are usually capitalized: names of deities, religions, religious followers, sacred books; words of family relationships used as names; particular places; nationalities and their languages, races, tribes; educational institutions, departments, degrees, particular courses; government departments, organizations, political parties; historical movements, periods, events, documents; specific electronic sources; and trade names.

PROPER NOUNS	COMMON NOUNS
God (used as a name)	a god
Book of Jeremiah	a sacred book
Grandmother Bishop	my grandmother
Father (used as a name)	my father
Lake Superior	a picturesque lake
the Capital Center	a center for the arts
the South	a southern state
Japan, a Japanese garden	an ornamental garden
University of Wisconsin	a good university
Geology 101	a geology course
Veterans Administration	a federal agency
Phi Kappa Psi	a fraternity
the Democratic Party	a political party
the Enlightenment	the eighteenth century
Great Depression	a recession
the Declaration of Independence	a treaty

PROPER NOUNS	COMMON NOUNS
the World Wide Web, the Web	a home page
the Internet, the Net	a computer network
Kleenex	a tissue

Months, holidays, and days of the week are capitalized: *May, Labor Day, Monday.* The seasons and numbers of the days of the month are not: *summer, the fifth of June.*

Names of school subjects are capitalized only if they are names of languages: *geology, history, English, French.* Names of particular courses are capitalized: *Geology 101, Principles of Economics.*

CAUTION: Do not capitalize common nouns to make them seem important: *Our company is currently hiring technical support staff* [not *Company, Technical Support Staff*].

22b Titles with proper names

Capitalize titles of persons when used as part of a proper name but usually not when used alone.

> Prof. Margaret Burnes; Dr. Harold Stevens; John Scott Williams Jr.; Anne Tilton, LL.D.
>
> District Attorney Mill was ruled out of order.
>
> The district attorney was elected for a two-year term.

Usage varies when the title of an important public figure is used alone: *The president* [or *President*] *vetoed the bill.*

22c Titles of works

In both titles and subtitles of works such as books, articles, and songs, major words should be capitalized. Minor words—articles, prepositions, and coordinating conjunctions—are not capitalized unless they are the first or last word of a title or subtitle.

> *The Impossible Theater: A Manifesto*
>
> "Man in the Middle"
>
> "I Want to Hold Your Hand"

22d First word of a sentence or quoted sentence

The first word of a sentence should of course be capitalized. Capitalize the first word of a quoted sentence but not a quoted phrase.

> In *Time* magazine Robert Hughes writes, "There are only about sixty Watteau paintings on whose authenticity all experts agree."

> Russell Baker has written that sports are "the opiate of the masses."

If a quoted sentence is interrupted by explanatory words, do not capitalize the first word after the interruption.

> "When we all think alike," he said, "no one is thinking."

22e First word following a colon

Do not capitalize the first word after a colon unless it begins an independent clause, in which case capitalization is optional.

> There is one glaring omission in the Bill of Rights: the right to vote.

> This we are forced to conclude: The [*or* the] federal government is needed to protect the rights of minorities.

22f Abbreviations

Capitalize abbreviations for departments and agencies of government, other organizations, and corporations; capitalize trade names and the call letters of radio and television stations.

> EPA, FBI, OPEC, IBM, Xerox, WCRB, KNBC-TV

ON THE WEB   dianahacker.com/pocket
► **Electronic grammar exercises**
  ► Mechanics
    ► Capital letters

23 | Abbreviations, numbers, and italics (underlining)

23a Abbreviations

Use abbreviations only when they are clearly appropriate.

Appropriate abbreviations. Feel free to use standard abbreviations for titles immediately before and after proper names.

TITLES BEFORE PROPER NAMES	TITLES AFTER PROPER NAMES
Mr. Ralph Meyer	Thomas Hines Jr.
Ms. Nancy Linehan	Anita Lor, Ph.D.
Dr. Margaret Simmons	Robert Simkowski, M.D.
Rev. John Stone	William Lyons, M.A.
St. Joan of Arc	Margaret Chin, LL.D
Prof. James Russo	Polly Stern, D.D.S.

Do not abbreviate a title if it is not used with a proper name: *My history professor* [not *prof.*] *was an expert on naval warfare.*

Familiar abbreviations for the names of organizations, corporations, and countries are also acceptable.

CIA, FBI, AFL-CIO, NAACP, IBM, UPI, CBS, USA

The CIA was established in 1947 by the National Security Act.

When using an unfamiliar abbreviation (such as NAB for National Association of Broadcasters) throughout a paper, write the full name followed by the abbreviation in parentheses at the first mention of the name. You may use the abbreviation alone from then on.

Other commonly accepted abbreviations include B.C., A.D., A.M., P.M., No., and $. The abbreviation B.C. ("before Christ") follows a date, and A.D. (*"anno Domini"*) precedes a date. Acceptable alternatives are B.C.E. ("before the common era") and C.E. ("common era").

40 B.C. (or 40 B.C.E.)   4:00 A.M. (or a.m.)   No. 12 (or no. 12)
A.D. 44 (or 44 C.E.)   6:00 P.M. (or p.m.) $150

Do not use these abbreviations, however, when they are not accompanied by a specific figure: *We set off for the lake early in the morning* [not *A.M.*].

Inappropriate abbreviations.   In formal writing, abbreviations for the following are not commonly accepted.

> **PERSONAL NAME**   Charles [*not* Chas.]
>
> **UNITS OF MEASUREMENT**   pound [*not* lb.]
>
> **DAYS OF THE WEEK**   Monday [*not* Mon.]
>
> **HOLIDAYS**   Christmas [*not* Xmas]
>
> **MONTHS**   January, February [*not* Jan., Feb.]
>
> **COURSES OF STUDY**   political science [*not* poli. sci.]
>
> **DIVISIONS OF WRITTEN WORKS**   chapter, page [*not* ch., p.]
>
> **STATES AND COUNTRIES**   Florida [*not* FL or Fla.]
>
> **PARTS OF A BUSINESS NAME**   Adams Lighting Company [*not* Adams Lighting Co.]; Kim and Brothers, Inc. [*not* Kim and Bros., Inc.]

Although Latin abbreviations are appropriate in footnotes and bibliographies and in informal writing, use the appropriate English phrases in formal writing.

> cf. (Latin *confer,* "compare")
>
> e.g. (Latin *exempli gratia,* "for example")
>
> et al. (Latin *et alii,* "and others")
>
> etc. (Latin *et cetera,* "and so forth")
>
> i.e. (Latin *id est,* "that is")
>
> N.B. (Latin *nota bene,* "note well")

23b Numbers

Spell out numbers of one or two words. Use figures for numbers that require more than two words to spell out.

> ▶ The 1980 eruption of Mount St. Helens blasted
>   ash ~~12~~ *twelve* miles into the sky and devastated ~~two
>   hundred thirty~~ *230* miles of land.

EXCEPTION: In technical and some business writing, figures are preferred even when spellings would be brief, but usage varies.

If a sentence begins with a number, spell out the number or rewrite the sentence.

> *One hundred fifty*
> ▶ ~~150~~ children in our program need expensive
>   ^
> dental treatment.

Generally, figures are acceptable for the following.

    DATES   July 4, 1776, 56 B.C., A.D. 30

    ADDRESSES   77 Latches Lane, 519 West 42nd Street

    PERCENTAGES   55 percent (or 55%)

    FRACTIONS, DECIMALS $1/2$, 0.047

    SCORES   7 to 3, 21–18

    STATISTICS   average age 37

    SURVEYS   4 out of 5

    EXACT AMOUNTS OF MONEY $105.37, $0.05

    DIVISIONS OF BOOKS   volume 3, chapter 4, page 189

    DIVISIONS OF PLAYS   Act I, scene i (or Act 1, scene 1)

    IDENTIFICATION NUMBERS   serial no. 1098

    TIME OF DAY   4:00 P.M., 1:30 A.M.

23c Italics (underlining)

In handwritten or typed papers, <u>underlining</u> represents *italics*, a slanting typeface used in printed material.

Titles of works.   Titles of the following works are italicized or underlined.

    TITLES OF BOOKS   *The Great Gatsby, A Distant Mirror*

    MAGAZINES   *Time, Scientific American*

    NEWSPAPERS   the *St. Louis Post-Dispatch*

    PAMPHLETS   *Common Sense, Facts about Marijuana*

    LONG POEMS   *The Waste Land, Paradise Lost*

    PLAYS   *King Lear, A Raisin in the Sun*

    FILMS   *Seabiscuit, Casablanca*

    TELEVISION PROGRAMS   *Will and Grace, 60 Minutes*

RADIO PROGRAMS	*All Things Considered*
MUSICAL COMPOSITIONS	Gershwin's *Porgy and Bess*
CHOREOGRAPHIC WORKS	Twyla Tharp's *Brief Fling*
WORKS OF VISUAL ART	Rodin's *The Thinker*
COMIC STRIPS	*Dilbert*
SOFTWARE	*WordPerfect, Acrobat Reader*
WEB SITES	*Barron's Online*

The titles of other works, such as short stories, essays, songs, and short poems, are enclosed in quotation marks. (See p. 80.)

NOTE: Do not use underlining or italics when referring to the Bible; titles of books in the Bible (Genesis, not *Genesis*); the titles of legal documents (the Constitution, not the *Constitution*); or the titles of your own papers.

Names of ships, trains, aircraft, spacecraft. Italicize or underline names of specific ships, trains, aircraft, and spacecraft.

> *Challenger, Spirit of St. Louis, Queen Elizabeth II, Silver Streak*

▶ The success of the Soviets' <u>Sputnik</u> galvanized the

U.S. space program.

Foreign words. Italicize or underline foreign words used in an English sentence.

▶ Instead of adhering to standard research protocol,

I decided to establish my own <u>modus operandi</u>.

EXCEPTION: Do not italicize or underline foreign words that have become part of the English language—"laissez-faire," "fait accompli," "habeas corpus," and "per diem," for example.

Words as words, etc. Italicize or underline words used as words, letters mentioned as letters, and numbers mentioned as numbers.

▶ Tomás assured us that the chemicals could

probably be safely mixed, but his <u>probably</u> stuck

in our minds.

▶ Speakers of some dialects have trouble

pronouncing the letter <u>r</u>.

▶ A big <u>3</u> was painted on the door to the lab.

NOTE: Quotation marks may be used instead of italics or underlining to set off words mentioned as words. (See p. 80.)

Inappropriate underlining. Underlining to emphasize words or ideas is distracting and should be used sparingly.

▶ Surfing the Internet can become an <u>addiction</u>.

ON THE WEB | dianahacker.com/pocket
▶ **Electronic grammar exercises**
  ▶ Mechanics
    ▶ Numbers and italics (underlining)

---

24 | Spelling and the hyphen

24a Spelling

A word processor equipped with a spell checker is a useful tool, but be aware of its limitations. A spell checker will not tell you how to spell words not listed in its dictionary; nor will it help you catch words commonly confused, such as *accept* and *except,* or common typographical errors, such as *own* for *won.* You will still need to proofread, and for some words you may need to turn to the dictionary.

NOTE: To check for correct use of commonly confused words (*accept* and *except, its* and *it's,* and so on), consult section 44, the Glossary of Usage.

Major spelling rules. If you need to improve your spelling, review the following rules and exceptions.

1. Use *i* before *e* except after *c* or when sounded like "ay," as in *neighbor* and *weigh*.

I BEFORE *E*   relieve, believe, sieve, niece, fierce, frieze

E BEFORE *I*   receive, deceive, sleigh, freight, eight

EXCEPTIONS   seize, either, weird, height, foreign, leisure

2. Generally, drop a final silent *-e* when adding a suffix that begins with a vowel. Keep the final *-e* if the suffix begins with a consonant.

desire, desiring   achieve, achievement

remove, removable   care, careful

Words such as *changeable, judgment, argument,* and *truly* are exceptions.

3. When adding *-s* or *-ed* to words ending in *-y,* ordinarily change *-y* to *-i* when the *-y* is preceded by a consonant but not when it is preceded by a vowel.

comedy, comedies   monkey, monkeys

dry, dried   play, played

With proper names ending in *-y,* however, do not change the *-y* to *-i* even if it is preceded by a consonant: *the Dougherty family, the Doughertys.*

4. If a final consonant is preceded by a single vowel *and* the consonant ends a one-syllable word or a stressed syllable, double the consonant when adding a suffix beginning with a vowel.

bet, betting   occur, occurrence

commit, committed

5. Add *-s* to form the plural of most nouns; add *-es* to singular nouns ending in *-s, -sh, -ch,* and *-x.*

table, tables   church, churches

paper, papers   dish, dishes

Ordinarily add -*s* to nouns ending in -*o* when the -*o* is preceded by a vowel. Add -*es* when it is preceded by a consonant.

radio, radios   hero, heroes

video, videos   tomato, tomatoes

To form the plural of a hyphenated compound word, add the -*s* to the chief word even if it does not appear at the end.

mother-in-law, mothers-in-law

NOTE: English words derived from other languages such as Latin or French sometimes form the plural as they would in their original language.

medium, media   chateau, chateaux

criterion, criteria

Spelling variations. Following is a list of some common words spelled differently in American and British English. Consult a dictionary for others.

AMERICAN	BRITISH
canceled, traveled	cancelled, travelled
color, humor	colour, humour
judgment	judgement
check	cheque
realize, apologize	realise, apologise
defense	defence
anemia, anesthetic	anaemia, anaesthetic
theater, center	theatre, centre
fetus	foetus
mold, smolder	mould, smoulder
civilization	civilisation
connection, inflection	connexion, inflexion
licorice	liquorice

24b The hyphen

In addition to the following guidelines, a dictionary will help you make decisions about hyphenation.

Compound words. The dictionary will tell whether to treat a compound word as a hyphenated compound (*water-repellent*), one word (*waterproof*), or two words (*water table*). If the compound word is not in the dictionary, treat it as two words.

▶ The prosecutor chose not to cross-examine any witnesses.

▶ The poet kept a small note book on his nightstand so that he could record his dreams.

▶ Alice walked through the looking/glass into a backward world.

Words functioning together as an adjective.   When two or more words function together as an adjective before a noun, connect them with a hyphen. Generally, do not use a hyphen when such compounds follow the noun.

▶ Pat Hobbs is not yet a well-known candidate.

▶ After our television campaign, Pat Hobbs will be well/known.

Do not use a hyphen to connect *-ly* adverbs to the words they modify.

▶ A slowly/moving truck tied up traffic.

NOTE: In a series, hyphens are suspended: *Do you prefer first-, second-, or third-class tickets?*

Conventional uses.   Hyphenate the written form of fractions and of compound numbers from twenty-one to ninety-nine. Also use the hyphen with the prefixes *all-, ex-,* and *self-* and with the suffix *-elect.*

▶ One-fourth of my income goes for rent.

▶ The charity is funding more self-help projects.

Division of a word at the end of a line.   If a word must be divided at the end of a line, use these guidelines:

1. Divide words between syllables.

2. Never divide one-syllable words.
3. Never divide a word so that a single letter stands alone at the end of a line or fewer than three letters begin a line.
4. When dividing a compound word at the end of a line, either make the break between the words that form the compound or put the whole word on the next line.

Division of an Internet address (or URL).   If you mention a URL in the text of your paper, divide it at some convenient point, such as after a slash or before a dot. Do not insert a hyphen to divide a URL; a reader could mistake the hyphen for part of the Internet address.

NOTE: When a URL appears in an MLA list of works cited, it must be divided after a slash. (See p. 141.)

ON THE WEB   dianahacker.com/pocket

► **Electronic grammar exercises**

  ► Mechanics

    ► The hyphen

This part of *A Pocket Style Manual* offers advice on the first steps in writing a research paper: posing a research question, finding appropriate sources, and evaluating those sources.

For help writing the actual paper—from forming a thesis to documenting your sources—consult one of the following color-coded sections, depending on the type of paper you have been assigned: MLA papers (red), APA papers (teal), or *Chicago*-style papers (blue).

25 Posing a research question

Working within the guidelines of your assignment, pose a few questions that seem worth researching. As you formulate possible questions, make sure that they are appropriate lines of inquiry for a research paper. Choose questions that are narrow (not too broad), challenging (not too bland), and grounded (not too speculative).

25a Choosing a narrow question

If your initial question is too broad, given the length of the paper you plan to write, look for ways to restrict your focus. Here, for example, is how two students narrowed their initial questions.

TOO BROAD

—What are the hazards of fad diets?

—What causes homelessness?

NARROWER

—What are the hazards of liquid diets?

—How has deinstitutionalization of the mentally ill contributed to the problem of homelessness?

25b Choosing a challenging question

Your research paper will be more interesting to both you and your audience if you base it on an intellectually challenging line of inquiry. Avoid bland questions that fail to provoke thought or engage readers in a debate.

TOO BLAND

—What is obsessive-compulsive disorder?

—Where is wind energy being used?

CHALLENGING

—What treatments for obsessive-compulsive disorder show the most promise?

—Does investing in wind energy make economic sense?

You may need to address a bland question in the course of answering a more challenging one, but it would be a mistake to use the bland question as the focus for the whole paper.

25c Choosing a grounded question

Finally, you will want to make sure that your research question is grounded, not too speculative. Although speculative questions—such as those that address philosophical, ethical, or religious issues—are worth asking and may receive some attention in a research paper, they are inappropriate central questions. The central argument of a research paper should be grounded in facts; it should not be based entirely on beliefs.

TOO SPECULATIVE

—Is capital punishment moral?

—What is the difference between a just and an unjust law?

GROUNDED

—Does capital punishment deter crime?

—Should we adjust federal laws so that penalties for possession of powdered cocaine and crack cocaine are comparable?

ON THE WEB   dianahacker.com/pocket

► **Electronic research exercises**
  ► Researching
    ► Research questions

26 Finding appropriate sources

Depending on your research question, some sources will prove more useful than others. For example, if your research question addresses a historical issue, you might look at reference works, books, scholarly articles, and primary sources such as speeches. If your research question addresses a current political issue, however, you might turn to magazine and newspaper articles, Web sites, and government documents.

| ON THE WEB | dianahacker.com/pocket |

▶ **Research and Documentation Online**
  ▶ Humanities/Social Sciences/History/Sciences
    ▶ Finding sources

26a Locating reference works

For some topics, you may want to begin your search by consulting general or specialized reference works. Check with a reference librarian to see which works are available in electronic format.

General reference works include encyclopedias, almanacs, atlases, and biographical references. Many specialized reference works are available: *Encyclopedia of Bioethics, Almanac of American Politics, The Historical and Cultural Atlas of African Americans,* and *The New Grove Dictionary of Music and Musicians,* to name a few.

26b Locating books

The books your library owns are listed in its computer catalog, along with other resources such as videos. You can search the catalog by author, title, or subject. Most of the time you will want to search by subject, using what is called a *keyword search.*

When a first search yields too few results, try searching by a broader topic. Then, once you find a book that looks on target, read the subject headings listed for it; they may be good search terms to try. When your search yields too many results, use the strategies for refining a search listed in the chart on page 105.

When a book looks promising, you can usually print out its bibliographic information, along with its call number. The call number is the book's address on the library shelf.

26c Locating articles

Libraries subscribe to a variety of electronic databases (sometimes called *periodical indexes*). Though these are usually accessed through an Internet browser, they provide quality sources that aren't available for free on the Web.

If you want to search for articles published before the 1980s, you may need to turn to a print index such as *Readers' Guide to Periodical Literature* or *Poole's Index to Periodical Literature*. A librarian can suggest other titles.

What databases offer.   Your library's databases will lead you to articles in newspapers, magazines, and scholarly or technical journals. Many databases also list sources such as scholarly reports, government documents, and dissertations.

Though each library is unique, here are some database services you may find available:

> *InfoTrac, EBSCOhost,* or *ProQuest.* Multidisciplinary databases containing newspaper, magazine, and journal articles.
>
> *FirstSearch.* Specialized databases leading to journal articles and library collections.
>
> *Lexis-Nexis.* A collection of databases particularly strong for current news and business and legal information.

Your library may also have specific databases that focus on a particular subject area, such as the following:

> *ERIC.* An education database.
>
> *MLA Bibliography.* A database of literary criticism.
>
> *MEDLINE.* A database of medical research.
>
> *PsycINFO.* A psychology research database.

Many databases include the full text of at least some articles; others list only citations or citations with short summaries called *abstracts*. When the full text is not available, the citation will give you enough information to track down an article.

How to search a database. To find articles on your topic in a database, you will most likely start with a keyword search. If the first keyword you try results in no matches, experiment with other terms. If you retrieve too many matches, narrow your search by using one of the strategies in the following chart.

REFINING SEARCHES IN DATABASES

Most electronic databases allow you to combine search terms in a variety of ways. The help feature of a database will give you specific advice about search techniques. Some of the most common ways to refine a search are listed here.

— Search for two or more terms:

apes AND language

— Search for a word string by putting it in quotation marks:

"American Sign Language"

— Search for any one of related terms:

"pygmy chimpanzee" OR bonobo OR Kanzi

— Exclude a term from a search:

bonobo NOT Kanzi

— Substitute a "wild card" symbol for letters that might vary:

synta* [to search for *syntax* or *syntactical*]

Many databases also allow you to restrict a search by date of publication (for example, within the last year).

26d Locating Web resources

For many topics, the Web is an excellent resource. For example, government agencies post information on the Web, and the sites of many organizations are filled with information about the issues they cover. Museums and libraries often post digital versions of primary sources, such as historical documents, on the Web.

NOTE: Many scholarly articles and other quality sources are not available for free on the Web. To access such articles at no cost, use a library database (see 26c).

Although the Web can be a rich source of information, it lacks quality control. As you probably know, anyone can publish on the Web, so you'll need to evaluate Web sources with special care (see 27c).

This section describes the following Web resources: search engines, directories, archives, government and news sites, and online discussions.

Search engines. Search engines such as *Google, AltaVista,* and *HotBot* take your search terms and seek matches among millions of Web pages. Often it is a good idea to try more than one search engine, since each locates sources in its own way. For current information about search engines, visit the following Web site, which classifies search engines, evaluates them, and provides updates on new search features:

> *Search Engine Watch*
> <http://www.searchenginewatch.com>

When using a search engine, focus your search as narrowly as possible to prevent getting an unmanageable number of matches (often called *hits*). Some of the most common ways to restrict a search are given in the following chart.

RESTRICTING SEARCHES IN WEB SEARCH ENGINES

Although search engines vary, most allow you to restrict a search in several ways. Some of the most common ways to restrict a search are listed here.

— Use combinations of keywords to search for sites containing two or more terms:

apes language Kanzi

— Use word strings, alone or in combination, to search for sites containing the exact strings:

"American Sign Language"
"American Sign Language" "pygmy chimpanzees"

— Exclude words from the search:

apes language NOT orangutan

— Restrict by date:

past six months

— Restrict by domain:

.edu [*or* .gov *or* .org]

— Restrict by keyword location:

in title [*or* in the URL]

Directories. Directories are put together by information specialists who arrange sites by topic: education, health, public issues, and so on. Many search engines, such as *Google,* offer a directory as an alternative means of conducting research.

Some directories are more selective and therefore more useful for scholarly research than the directories that typically accompany a search engine. The following list includes directories especially useful for scholarly research:

Infomine <http://infomine.ucr.edu>

Scout Report Archives <http://scout.wisc.edu/archives>

Librarian's Index to the Internet <http://www.lii.org>

World Wide Web Virtual Library <http://www.vlib.org>

Archives. Archives contain the texts of poems, books, speeches, political cartoons, and historically significant documents such as the Declaration of Independence. The following online archives are impressive collections:

American Memory <http://memory.loc.gov>

Avalon Project <http://www.yale.edu/lawweb/avalon/avalon.htm>

Electronic Text Center <http://etext.lib.virginia.edu>

Eurodocs <http://library.byu.edu/~rdh/eurodocs>

Internet History Sourcebooks <http://www.fordham.edu/halsall>

The Making of America <http://moa.umdl.umich.edu>

Government and news sites. For current topics, both government and news sites can prove useful. Many government agencies at every level provide online information. Government-maintained sites include resources such as facts and statistics, legal texts, reports, and searchable reference databases. Here are just a few government sites (notice that the last one will lead you to others):

Census Bureau <http://www.census.gov>

Fedstats <http://www.fedstats.gov>

Thomas Legislative Information <http://thomas.loc.gov>

United Nations <http://www.un.org>

U.S. Federal Government Agencies Directory <http://www.lib.lsu.edu/gov/fedgov.html>

Many news organizations offer up-to-date information on the Web. However, archived information may be available only for a fee; check with your library to see if it subscribes to a news archive that you can access at no charge. Following are a few useful news sites on the Web:

CNN <http://www.cnn.com>

Kidon Media-Link <http://www.kidon.com/medialink/index.html>

NewsLink <http://newslink.org>

New York Times <http://www.nytimes.com>

Online discussions.   Online discussion groups allow you to communicate with others who share an interest in your topic, but such discussions are not always a valid source for a research project. As a rule, do not use ideas or quotations from an online discussion unless the discussion is archived (saved in a permanent record).

Online discussions that do not take place in real time include e-mail discussion lists (sometimes called LISTSERVs), Usenet newsgroups, and bulletin boards. To find publicly available lists, go to one of these Web sites:

CataList <http://www.lsoft.com/catalist.html>

Topica <http://www.liszt.com>

Google Groups <http://groups.google.com/>

Real-time discussions include MUDs, MOOs, and chat rooms. Some are ongoing forums; others are set up to allow a group of people to communicate about a particular issue at a specific time.

27   Evaluating sources

With electronic search tools, you can often locate dozens or even hundreds of potential sources for your topic—far more than you will have time to read. Your challenge will be to select a reasonable number of quality sources that deserve your time and attention.

Later, once you have selected an array of sources, your challenge will be to read them with an open mind and a critical eye.

27a Selecting sources

Sections 26b–26d suggest how to restrict the number of "hits" that come up in a book catalog, a database, or a search engine. This section suggests how to scan through the lists of hits looking for those that seem most promising.

Scanning lists in a book catalog. The library's book catalog will usually give you a fairly short list of hits. A book's title and date of publication are often your first clues as to whether the book is worth consulting. If a title looks interesting, you can click on it for further information: the book's subject matter and its length, for example.

Scanning lists in a database. Most databases, such as those offered by *ProQuest* and *Lexis-Nexis,* provide at least the following information, which can help you decide if a source is relevant, current, scholarly enough, and neither too short nor too long for your purposes.

Title and brief description (How relevant?)

Date (How current?)

Name of periodical (How scholarly?)

Length (How extensive in coverage?)

Scanning lists in a search engine. Anyone can publish on the Web, and unreliable sites often masquerade as legitimate sources of information. As you scan through a list of hits, look for the following clues about the probable relevance, currency, and reliability of a site—but be prepared to be disappointed, as the clues are by no means foolproof.

Title, keywords, and lead-in text (How relevant?)

Date (How current?)

An indication of the site's sponsor or purpose (How reliable?)

The URL, especially the domain name (How relevant? How reliable?)

27b Reading with an open mind and a critical eye

As you begin reading the sources you have chosen, keep an open mind. Do not let your personal beliefs prevent you from listening to new ideas and opposing viewpoints. Your research question—not a snap judgment answer to the question—should guide your reading.

When you read critically, you are not necessarily judging an author's work harshly; you are simply checking for possible signs of bias and assessing the reliability of the writer's argument. Questions such as those in the following chart can help you weigh the strengths and weaknesses of the sources you read.

READING CRITICALLY

CHECKING FOR SIGNS OF BIAS

—Does the author or publisher have political leanings or religious views that could affect objectivity?

—Is the author or publisher associated with a special-interest group, such as Greenpeace or the National Rifle Association, that might see only one side of an issue?

—How fairly does the author treat opposing views?

—Does the author's language show signs of bias?

ASSESSING AN ARGUMENT

—What is the author's central claim or thesis?

—How does the author support this claim—with relevant and sufficient evidence or with just a few anecdotes or emotional examples?

—Are statistics accurate? Have they been used fairly?

—Are any of the author's assumptions questionable?

—Does the author consider opposing arguments and refute them persuasively?

27c Assessing Web sources with special care

Sophisticated-looking Web sites can be full of dubious information, and the identities of those who created a site are often hidden, along with their motives for having created it. In contrast, sites with reliable information can stand up to careful scrutiny. For a checklist on evaluating Web sources, see the next page.

EVALUATING WEB SOURCES

CAUTION: If the authorship and the sponsorship of a site are both un-clear, be extremely suspicious of the site.

AUTHORSHIP

—Is there an author? You may need to do some clicking and scrolling to find the author's name. Check the home page or an "about this site" link.

—Can you tell whether an author is knowledgeable and credible? Look for a home page, which may provide evidence of the author's expertise.

SPONSORSHIP

—Who, if anyone, sponsors the site? The sponsor of a site is often named and described on the home page.

—What does the domain name tell you? The domain name often specifies the type of group hosting the site: commercial (.com), educational (.edu), nonprofit (.org), governmental (.gov), military (.mil), or network (.net).

PURPOSE AND AUDIENCE

Why was the site created: To argue a position? To sell a product? To inform readers?

—Who is the site's intended audience?

CURRENCY

—How current is the site? Check for the date of publication or the latest update.

—How current are the site's links? If many of the links no longer work, the site may be too dated for your purposes.

MLA

Most assignments in English and other humanities classes are based to some extent on reading. At times you will be asked to respond to one, two, or a few readings—such as essays or literary works. At other times you may be asked to write a research paper that draws on a wide variety of sources.

English and humanities instructors will usually ask you to document your sources with the Modern Language Association (MLA) system of citations described in section 32. When writing a paper that draws on written sources, you face three main challenges in addition to documenting those sources: (1) supporting a thesis, (2) avoiding plagiarism, and (3) integrating quotations and other source material.

28 Supporting a thesis

Most assignments ask you to form a thesis, or main idea, and to support that thesis with well-organized evidence.

28a Forming a thesis

A thesis is a one-sentence (or occasionally a two-sentence) statement of your central idea. Usually your thesis will appear at the end of the first paragraph (as in the example on p. 151), but if you need to provide readers with considerable background information, you may place it at the end of the second paragraph.

Although the thesis appears early in your paper, do not attempt to write it until fairly late in your reading and writing process. Reading and rereading will sharpen your ideas. And writing about a subject is a way of learning about it; as you write, your understanding of your subject will almost certainly deepen. As writer E. M. Forster once put it, "How can I know what I think until I see what I say?"

Early in the reading and writing process, you can keep your mind open—yet focused—by posing questions. The thesis that you articulate later in the process will be an answer to the central question you pose, as in the following examples.

PUBLIC POLICY QUESTION

Should states regulate use of cell phones in moving vehicles?

POSSIBLE THESIS

States must regulate use of cell phones on the road because drivers using phones are seriously impaired and because laws on negligent and reckless driving are not sufficient to punish offenders.

LITERATURE QUESTION

What does Stephen Crane's short story "The Open Boat" reveal about the relationship between humans and nature?

POSSIBLE THESIS

In Stephen Crane's gripping tale "The Open Boat," four men lost at sea discover not only that nature is indifferent to their fate but that their own particular talents make little difference as they struggle for survival.

Notice that both thesis statements take a stand on a debatable issue—an issue about which intelligent, well-meaning people might disagree. Each writer's job will be to convince such people that his or her view is worth taking seriously.

ON THE WEB   dianahacker.com/pocket

▶ **Electronic research exercises**
   ▶ **MLA**
      ▶ Thesis statements in MLA papers

28b Organizing your evidence

The body of your paper will consist of evidence in support of your thesis. Early in the writing process, keep your organizational plan simple. Instead of constructing a formal outline, list your key lines of argument, as the student who wrote the first thesis on page 114 has done.

- Drivers distracted by cellular phones are seriously impaired.
- Current laws on negligent and reckless driving are not adequate.
- In the United States, major traffic laws must be passed on the state level.

Once you have drafted your paper, you may want to turn your list into a formal outline that reflects not only your key lines of argument but also the complexities of your evidence.

29 Avoiding plagiarism

Your research paper is a collaboration between you and your sources. To be fair and ethical, you must acknowledge your debt to the writers of those sources. If you don't, you are guilty of plagiarism, a serious academic offense.

Three different acts are considered plagiarism: (1) failing to cite quotations and borrowed ideas, (2) failing to enclose borrowed language in quotation marks, and (3) failing to put summaries and paraphrases in your own words.

29a Citing quotations and borrowed ideas

You must of course cite all direct quotations or other material taken directly from a source (for example, charts or cartoons). You must also cite any ideas borrowed from a source: an author's original insights, any information summarized or paraphrased from the text, and statistics and other specific facts.

The only exception is common knowledge—general information that your readers may know or could easily locate. For example, it is well known that Toni Morrison won the Nobel Prize in literature in 1993 and that Emily Dickinson published only a handful of poems during her life. As a rule, when you have seen certain information repeatedly in your reading, you don't need to cite it. However, when information has appeared in only a few sources, when it is highly specific (as with statistics), or when it is controversial, you should cite it.

The Modern Language Association recommends a system of in-text citations. Here, briefly, is how the MLA citation system usually works:

1. The source is introduced by a signal phrase that names its author.
2. The material being cited is followed by a page number in parentheses.
3. At the end of the paper, a list of works cited (arranged alphabetically according to authors' last names) gives complete publication information about the source.

IN-TEXT CITATION

According to Donald Redelmeier and Robert Tibshirani, "The use of cellular telephones in motor vehicles is associated with a quadrupling of the risk of a collision during the brief period of a call" (453).

ENTRY IN THE LIST OF WORKS CITED

Redelmeier, Donald A., and Robert J. Tibshirani. "Association between Cellular-Telephone Calls and Motor Vehicle Collisions." New England Journal of Medicine 336 (1997): 453-58.

Handling an MLA citation is not always this simple. For a detailed discussion of possible variations, see 32.

29b Enclosing borrowed language in quotation marks

To show readers that you are using a source's exact phrases or sentences, enclose them in quotation marks unless they have been set off from the text (see p. 122). To omit the quotation marks is to claim—falsely—that the language is your own. Such an omission is plagiarism even if you have cited the source.

ORIGINAL SOURCE

Future cars will provide drivers with concierge services, web-based information, online e-mail capabilities, CD-ROM access, on-screen and audio navigation technology, and a variety of other information and entertainment services.

–Matt Sundeen, "Cell Phones and Highway Safety: 2000 State Legislative Update," p. 1

PLAGIARISM

Matt Sundeen points out that in cars of the future drivers will have concierge services, web-based information, online e-mail capabilities,

CD-ROM access, on-screen and audio navigation technology, and a variety of other information and entertainment services (1).

BORROWED LANGUAGE IN QUOTATION MARKS

Matt Sundeen points out that in cars of the future drivers will have "concierge services, web-based information, online e-mail capabilities, CD-ROM access, on-screen and audio navigation technology, and a variety of other information and entertainment services" (1).

29c Putting summaries and paraphrases in your own words

A summary condenses information from a source; a paraphrase conveys this information in about the same number of words. When you summarize or paraphrase, it is not enough to name the source; you must restate the source's meaning using your own language. You are guilty of plagiarism if you half-copy the author's sentences — either by mixing the author's phrases with your own without using quotation marks or by plugging your synonyms into the author's sentence structure.

The first paraphrase of the following source is plagiarized — even though the source is cited — because too much of its language is borrowed from the original. The underlined strings of words have been copied word-for-word (without quotation marks). In addition, the writer has closely echoed the sentence structure of the source, merely plugging in some synonyms (*demonstrated* for *shown, devising* for *designing,* and *car* for *automotive*).

ORIGINAL SOURCE

The automotive industry has not shown good judgment in designing automotive features that distract drivers. A classic example is the use of a touch-sensitive screen to replace all the controls for radios, tape/CD players, and heating/cooling. Although an interesting technology, such devices require that the driver take his eyes off the road.

–Tom Magliozzi and Ray Magliozzi, Letter to a Massachusetts state senator, p. 3

PLAGIARISM: UNACCEPTABLE BORROWING

Radio show hosts Tom and Ray Magliozzi argue that <u>the automotive industry has not</u> demonstrated <u>good judgment in</u> devising car <u>features that distract drivers.</u> One feature is <u>a touch-sensitive screen</u> that

replaces <u>controls for radios, tape/CD players, and heating/cooling.</u>
Although the technology is interesting, <u>such devices require that</u> a
driver look away from the road (3).

To avoid plagiarizing an author's language, resist
the temptation to look at the source while you are summarizing or paraphrasing—or to download the source
and try to change the author's wording. Instead, put the
source aside, write from memory or rough notes, and
check later for accuracy.

ACCEPTABLE PARAPHRASE

Radio show hosts Tom and Ray Magliozzi claim that motor vehicle
manufacturers do not always design features with safety in mind. For
example, when designers replaced radio, CD player, and temperature
control knobs with touch-sensitive panels, they were forgetting one
thing: To use the panels, drivers would need to take their eyes off
the road (3).

ON THE WEB   dianahacker.com/pocket

▶ **Electronic research exercises**
   ▶ MLA
      ▶ Avoiding plagiarism in MLA papers

ON THE WEB   dianahacker.com/pocket

▶ **Electronic research exercises**
   ▶ MLA
      ▶ Recognizing common knowledge in MLA papers

---

30 Integrating nonfiction sources

By carefully integrating quotations and other source
material into your own text, you help readers understand whose views you are hearing—yours or those of
your sources. In addition, you show readers where cited
material begins and where it ends.

NOTE: When using the Modern Language Association's
in-text citations, use present tense or present perfect
tense verbs in phrases that introduce quotations or other

source material from nonfiction sources: *Perry points out that* or *Perry has pointed out that* (not *Perry pointed out that*). If you have good reason to emphasize that the author's language or opinion was articulated in the past, however, the past tense is acceptable.

The first time you mention an author, use the full name: *Matt Sundeen reports that. . . .* when you refer to the author again, you may use the last name only: *Sundeen summarizes the statistics.*

30a Integrating quotations

Readers need to move from your own words to the words of a source without feeling a jolt.

Using signal phrases.   Avoid dropping quotations into the text without warning. Instead, provide clear signal phrases, usually including the author's name, to prepare readers for a quotation.

DROPPED QUOTATION

In 2000, the legislature of Suffolk County passed a law restricting drivers' use of handheld phones. "The bill prohibits the use of a cell phone while driving unless it is equipped with an earpiece or can act like a speakerphone, leaving the driver's hands free" (Kelley 1).

QUOTATION WITH SIGNAL PHRASE

In 2000, the legislature of Suffolk County passed a law restricting drivers' use of handheld phones. According to journalist Tina Kelley, "The bill prohibits the use of a cell phone while driving unless it is equipped with an earpiece or can act like a speakerphone, leaving the driver's hands free" (1).

To avoid monotony, try to vary both the language and the placement of your signal phrases.

> In the words of researchers Redelmeier and Tibshirani, " . . . "
>
> As Matt Sundeen has noted, " . . . "
>
> Patti Pena, mother of a child killed by a driver distracted by a cell phone, points out that " . . . "
>
> " . . . ," writes Christine Haughney, " . . . "
>
> " . . . ," claims wireless industry spokesperson Annette Jacobs.
>
> Radio hosts Tom and Ray Magliozzi offer a persuasive counterargument: " . . . "

When your signal phrase includes a verb, choose one that is appropriate in the context. Is your source arguing a point, making an observation, reporting a fact, drawing a conclusion, refuting an argument, or stating a belief? By choosing an appropriate verb, such as one on the following list, you can make your source's stance clear.

acknowledges	comments	endorses	reasons
adds	compares	grants	refutes
admits	confirms	illustrates	rejects
agrees	contends	implies	reports
argues	declares	insists	responds
asserts	denies	notes	suggests
believes	disputes	observes	thinks
claims	emphasizes	points out	writes

Limiting your use of quotations. Except for the following legitimate uses of quotations, use your own words to summarize and paraphrase your sources and to explain your own ideas.

WHEN TO USE QUOTATIONS

— When language is especially vivid or expressive

— When exact wording is needed for technical accuracy

— When it is important to let the debaters of an issue explain their positions in their own words

— When the words of an important authority lend weight to an argument

— When the language of a source is the topic of your discussion (as in an analysis or interpretation)

It is not always necessary to quote full sentences from a source. To reduce your reliance on the words of others, you can often integrate a phrase from a source into your own sentence structure.

Redelmeier and Tibshirani found that hands-free phones were not any safer in vehicles than other cell phones. They suggest that crashes involving cell phones may "result from a driver's limitations with regard to attention rather than dexterity" (456).

Using the ellipsis mark. To condense a quoted passage, you can use the ellipsis mark (three spaced periods) to indicate that you have omitted words. What remains must be grammatically complete.

The University of North Carolina Highway Safety Research Center has begun a study assessing a variety of driver distractions. According to Allyson Vaughan, "The research . . . is intended to inject some empirical evidence into the debate over whether talking on wireless phones while driving leads to accidents" (1).

The writer has omitted the words *funded by the AAA Foundation for Traffic Safety,* which appeared in the source.

On the rare occasions when you want to omit a full sentence or more, use a period before the three ellipsis dots.

Redelmeier and Tibshirani acknowledge that their study "indicates an association but not necessarily a causal relation between the use of cellular telephones while driving and a subsequent motor vehicle collision. . . . In addition, our study did not include serious injuries . . ." (457).

Ordinarily, do not use an ellipsis mark at the beginning or at the end of a quotation. Your readers will understand that the quoted material is taken from a longer passage, so such marks are not necessary. The only exception occurs when words at the end of the final quoted sentence have been dropped. In such cases, put three ellipsis dots before the closing quotation mark and parenthetical reference, as in the previous example.

Obviously you should not use an ellipsis mark to distort the meaning of your source.

Using brackets. Brackets (square parentheses) allow you to insert words of your own into quoted material. You can insert words in brackets to clarify matters or to keep a sentence grammatical in your context.

According to economists Robert Hahn and Paul Tetlock, "Some studies say they [hands-free phones] would have no impact on accidents, while others suggest the reductions could be sizable" (2).

To indicate an error in a quotation, insert [sic] right after the error or (sic) after the closing quotation mark.

Setting off long quotations.   When you quote more than four typed lines of prose, set off the quotation by indenting it one inch (or ten spaces) from the left margin.

Long quotations should be introduced by an informative sentence, usually followed by a colon. Quotation marks are unnecessary because the indented format tells readers that the words are taken directly from the source.

Tom and Ray Magliozzi are not impressed by economists who conduct risk-benefit analyses of phone use by drivers:

> Other critics [of regulation of cell phones]--some from presti-
> gious "think tanks"--perform what appear to be erudite
> cost/benefit analyses. The problem here is that the benefits
> are always in units of convenience and productivity while
> the costs are in units of injuries and people's lives! (2)

At the end of an indented quotation the parenthetical citation goes outside the final punctuation mark.

30b Integrating summaries and paraphrases

Summaries and paraphrases are written in your own words. As with quotations, you should introduce most summaries and paraphrases with a signal phrase that names the author and places the material in context. Readers will then understand that everything between the signal phrase and the parenthetical citation summarizes or paraphrases the cited source.

Without the signal phrase (underlined) in the following example, readers might think that only the quotation at the end is being cited, when in fact the whole paragraph is based on the source.

<u>Alasdair Cain and Mark Burris report that</u> research on traffic accidents and cell phone use has been inconclusive. Many factors play a role: for example, the type of phone (hands-free or not), the extent to which the conversation is distracting, and the demographic profile of the driver. Although research suggests that phoning in a moving vehicle affects driver performance, studies have failed to quantify the degree of driver impairment. Cain and Burris write that drivers using cell phones on the road "were anywhere from 34 percent to 300 percent more likely to have an accident" (1).

When the context makes clear where the cited material begins, however, you may omit the signal phrase and name the author in the parentheses.

30c Integrating statistics and other facts

When you are citing a statistic or other specific fact, a signal phrase is often not necessary. In most cases, readers will understand that the citation refers to the statistic or fact (not the whole paragraph).

As of 2000, there were about ninety million cell phone users in the United States, with 85% of them using their phones while on the road (Sundeen 1).

There is nothing wrong, however, with using a signal phrase to introduce a statistic or other fact.

Matt Sundeen reports that as of 2000, there were about ninety million cell phone users in the United States, with 85% of them using their phones while on the road (1).

ON THE WEB	dianahacker.com/pocket

▶ **Electronic research exercises**
  ▶ MLA
    ▶ Integrating quotations in MLA papers

31 Integrating literary quotations

Integrating quotations from a literary work smoothly into your own text can present a challenge. Because of the complexities of literature, do not be surprised to find yourself puzzling over the most graceful way to tuck in a short phrase or the clearest way to introduce a more extended passage from the work.

NOTE: The parenthetical citations at the ends of examples in this section tell readers where the quoted words can be found. They indicate the lines of a poem; the act, scene, and lines of a play; or the page number of a quotation from a short story or novel. (For guidelines on citing literary works, see pp. 133–34.)

31a Introducing literary quotations

When writing about nonfiction essays and books, you have probably learned to introduce a quotation with a signal phrase naming the author: *According to Jane Doe, Jane Doe points out that,* and so on.

When introducing quotations from a literary work, however, make sure that you don't confuse the work's author with the narrator of a story, the speaker of a poem, or a character in a play. Instead of naming the author, you can refer to the narrator or speaker—or to the work itself.

INAPPROPRIATE

Poet Andrew Marvell describes his fear of death like this: "But at my back I always hear/Time's wingèd chariot hurrying near" (21-22).

APPROPRIATE

Addressing his beloved in an attempt to win her sexual favors, the speaker of the poem argues that death gives them no time to waste: "But at my back I always hear/Time's wingèd chariot hurrying near" (21-22).

APPROPRIATE

The poem "To His Coy Mistress" says as much about fleeting time and death as it does about sexual passion. Its most powerful lines may well be "But at my back I always hear/Time's wingèd chariot hurrying near" (21-22).

In the last example, you could of course mention the author as well: *Marvell's poem "To His Coy Mistress" says as much....* Although the author is mentioned, he is not being confused with the speaker of the poem.

If you are quoting the words of a character in a story or a play, you should name the character who is speaking and provide a context for the spoken words. In the following example, the quoted dialogue is from Tennessee Williams's play *The Glass Menagerie.*

Laura's life is so completely ruled by Amanda that when urged to make a wish on the moon, she asks, "What shall I wish for, Mother?" (1.5.140).

For examples of quoted dialogue from a short story, see page 153.

31b Avoiding shifts in tense

Because it is conventional to write about literature in the present tense (see p. 35) and because literary works often use other tenses, you will need to exercise some care when weaving quotations into your own text. A first-draft attempt may result in an awkward shift, as it did for one student who was writing about Nadine Gordimer's short story "Friday's Footprint."

TENSE SHIFT

When Rita sees Johnny's relaxed attitude, "she blushed, like a wave of illness" (159).

To avoid the distracting shift from present to past tense, the writer decided to include the reference to Rita's blushing in her own text and reduce the length of the quotation.

REVISED

When Rita sees Johnny's relaxed attitude, she blushes, "like a wave of illness" (159).

The writer could have changed the quotation to present tense, using brackets to indicate the change, like this: *When Rita sees Johnny's relaxed attitude, "she blushe[s], like a wave of illness" (159).* (See also p. 121.)

31c Formatting literary quotations

Guidelines for formatting quotations from short stories or novels, poems, and plays are slightly different from one another.

Short stories or novels.   If a quotation from a short story or a novel takes up four or fewer typed lines, put it in quotation marks and run it into the text of your essay. Include a page number in parentheses after the quotation.

The narrator of Eudora Welty's "Why I Live at the P.O.," known to us only as "Sister," makes many catty remarks about her enemies. For example, she calls Mr. Whitaker "this photographer with the pop-eyes" (46).

If a quotation from a short story or a novel is five typed lines or longer, set it off from the text by indenting one inch (or ten spaces) from the left margin; when you set a quotation off from the text, do not use quotation marks. (See also p. 122.) Put the page number in parentheses after the final mark of punctuation.

Sister's tale begins with "I," and she makes every event revolve around herself, even her sister's marriage:

> I was getting along fine with Mama, Papa-Daddy, and
> Uncle Rondo until my sister Stella-Rondo just separated
> from her husband and came back home again. Mr. Whitaker!
> Of course I went with Mr. Whitaker first, when he first
> appeared here in China Grove, taking "Pose Yourself"
> photos, and Stella-Rondo broke us up. (46)

Poems. Enclose quotations of three or fewer lines of poetry in quotation marks within your text, and indicate line breaks with a slash. Include line numbers in parentheses at the end of the quotation. For the first reference, use the word "lines." Thereafter, use just numbers.

The opening of Frost's "Fire and Ice" strikes a conversational tone: "Some say the world will end in fire, / Some say in ice" (lines 1-2).

When you quote four or more lines of poetry, set the quotation off from the text by indenting one inch (or ten spaces) and omit the quotation marks. Put the line numbers in parentheses after the final mark of punctuation.

Like the rest of the poem, the final stanza of Louise Bogan's "Women" presents a negative stereotype of women, suggesting that women tend to be too timid and housebound to embrace life fully:

> They hear in every whisper that speaks to them
> A shout and a cry.
> As like as not, when they take life over their door-sills
> They should let it go by. (17-20)

NOTE: You may reduce the one-inch indent to make the lines fit.

Plays. If a quotation from a character in a play takes up four or fewer typed lines, put quotation marks around it and run it into the text of your essay. Whenever possible, include the act, scene, and line numbers in parentheses at the end of the quotation. Separate the numbers with periods, and use arabic numerals unless your instructor prefers roman numerals.

Two attendants silently watch as the sleepwalking Lady Macbeth subconsciously struggles with her guilt: "Here's the smell of blood still. All the perfumes of Arabia will not sweeten this little hand" (5.1.50-51).

32   MLA documentation style

To document sources, the Modern Language Association (MLA) recommends in-text citations that refer readers to a list of works cited.

ON THE WEB   dianahacker.com/pocket
▶ **Electronic research exercises**
  ▶ MLA
    ▶ MLA documentation

32a MLA in-text citations

MLA in-text citations are made with a combination of signal phrases and parenthetical references. A signal phrase indicates that something taken from a source (a quotation, summary, paraphrase, or fact) is about to be used; usually the signal phrase includes the author's name. The parenthetical reference, which comes after the cited material, normally includes at least a page number. In the following models, the elements of the in-text citation are shown in color.

IN-TEXT CITATION

One driver, Peter Cohen, says that after he was rear-ended, the guilty party emerged from his vehicle still talking on the phone (127).

Readers can look up the author's last name in the alphabetized list of works cited, where they will learn the work's title and other publication information. When readers decide to consult the source, the page number will take them to the passage that has been cited.

NOTE: If your cited material runs to more than one page, give the range of pages (such as 235–36 or 399–400).

Basic rules for print and electronic sources.   The MLA system of in-text citations, which depends heavily on authors' names and page numbers, was created in the early 1980s with print sources in mind. Because some of today's electronic sources have unclear authorship and lack page numbers, they present a challenge. Nevertheless, the rules for print and electronic sources are the same.

The models in this section (items 1–5) show how the MLA system usually works and explain what to do if your source has no author or page numbers.

1. **AUTHOR NAMED IN A SIGNAL PHRASE**   Ordinarily, introduce the material being cited with a signal phrase that names

the author. In addition to preparing readers for the source, the signal phrase allows you to keep the parenthetical citation brief.

Christine Haughney reports that shortly after Japan made it illegal to use a handheld phone while driving, "accidents caused by using the phones dropped by 75 percent" (A8).

The signal phrase—"Christine Haughney reports that"— names the author; the parenthetical citation gives the page number of the newspaper article in which the quoted words may be found.

Notice that the period follows the parenthetical citation. When a quotation ends with a question mark or an exclamation point, leave the end punctuation inside the quotation mark and add a period after the parentheses: ". . . ?" (8). See page 126 for an exception to this rule.

2. **AUTHOR NAMED IN PARENTHESES** If a signal phrase does not name the author, put the author's last name in parentheses along with the page number.

Most states do not keep adequate records on the number of times cell phones are a factor in accidents; as of December 2000, only ten states were trying to keep such records (Sundeen 2).

3. **AUTHOR UNKNOWN** Use the complete title in a signal phrase or give a short form of the title in parentheses. Titles of books are underlined; titles of articles and other short works are put in quotation marks.

As of 2001, at least three hundred towns and municipalities had considered legislation regulating use of cell phones while driving ("Lawmakers" 2).

NOTE: Often the name of the author of a Web source is available but hard to find. For example, it may appear at the end of the document or on the site's home page.

If a source has no known author but was prepared by a corporate entity, such as an organization or a government agency, name the corporate entity as the author (see item 9 on p. 131).

4. **PAGE NUMBER UNKNOWN** You may omit the page number if a work lacks page numbers, as is the case with many Web sources. Although printouts from Web sites usually show page numbers, printers don't always provide the

same page breaks; for this reason, MLA recommends treating such sources as unpaginated.

The California Highway Patrol opposes restrictions on the use of phones while driving, claiming that distracted drivers can already be prosecuted (Jacobs).

According to Jacobs, the California Highway Patrol opposes restrictions on the use of phones while driving, claiming that distracted drivers can already be prosecuted.

When the pages of a Web source are stable (as in PDF files), however, supply a page number in your in-text citation.

NOTE: If a Web source numbers its paragraphs or screens, give the abbreviation "par." or "pars." or the word "screen" or "screens" in the parentheses: (Smith, par. 4).

5. ONE-PAGE SOURCE   If the source is one page long, MLA allows (but does not require) you to omit the page number. Many instructors will want you to supply the page number because without it readers may not know where your citation ends or, worse yet, may not realize that you have provided a citation at all.

In the following example, a page number is given for a one-page source.

Milo Ippolito reports that the driver who struck and killed a two-year-old while using her cell phone got off with a light sentence even though she left the scene of the accident and failed to call 911 for help (J1). In this and in similar cases, traffic offenders distracted by cell phones have not been sufficiently punished under current laws.

Variations on the basic rules.   This section describes the MLA guidelines for handling a variety of situations not covered by the basic rules just given.

6. TWO OR MORE TITLES BY THE SAME AUTHOR   If your list of works cited includes two or more titles by the same author, mention the title of the work in the signal phrase or include a short version of the title in the parentheses.

On December 6, 2000, reporter Jamie Stockwell wrote that distracted driver Jason Jones had been charged with "two counts of vehicular manslaughter . . . in the deaths of John and Carole Hall" ("Phone" B1). The next day Stockwell reported the judge's ruling: Jones "was convicted of negligent driving and fined $500, the maximum penalty allowed" ("Man" B4).

Titles of articles and other short works are placed in quotation marks, as in the example just given. Titles of books are underlined.

When both the author's name and a short title appear in parentheses, separate them with a comma.

According to police reports, there were no skid marks indicating that the distracted driver who killed John and Carole Hall had even tried to stop (Stockwell, "Man" B4).

7. TWO OR THREE AUTHORS   Name the authors in the signal phrase, as in the following example, or include their last names in the parenthetical reference: (Redelmeier and Tibshirani 453).

Redelmeier and Tibshirani found that "the risk of a collision when using a cellular telephone was four times higher than the risk when a cellular telephone was not being used" (453).

When three authors are named in the parentheses, separate the names with commas: (Alton, Davies, and Rice 56).

8. FOUR OR MORE AUTHORS   Name all of the authors or include only the first author's name followed by "et al." (Latin for "and others"). Make sure that your citation matches the entry in the list of works cited (see also item 2 on p. 137).

The study was extended for two years, and only after results were reviewed by an independent panel did the researchers publish their findings (Blaine et al. 35).

9. CORPORATE AUTHOR   When the author is a corporation, an organization, or a government agency, name the corporate author either in the signal phrase or in the parentheses.

Researchers at the Harvard Center for Risk Analysis found that the risks of driving while phoning were small compared with other driving risks (3-4).

In the list of works cited, the Harvard Center for Risk Analysis is treated as the author and alphabetized under *H*.

NOTE: When a government agency is treated as the author, it will be alphabetized in the list of works cited under the name of the government, such as "United States." For this reason, you must name the government in your in-text citation: *The United States Department of Transportation reports that. . . .*

10. AUTHORS WITH THE SAME LAST NAME   If your list of works cited includes works by authors with the same last name, include the author's first name in the signal phrase or first initial in the parentheses.

Estimates of the number of accidents caused by distracted drivers

vary because little evidence is being collected (D. Smith 7).

11. INDIRECT SOURCE (SOURCE QUOTED IN ANOTHER SOURCE)   When a writer's or a speaker's quoted words appear in a source written by someone else, begin the citation with the abbreviation "qtd. in."

According to Richard Retting, "As the comforts of home and the

efficiency of the office creep into the automobile, it is becoming

increasingly attractive as a work space" (qtd. in Kilgannon A23).

12. ENCYCLOPEDIA OR DICTIONARY   Unless an encyclopedia or a dictionary has an author, it will be alphabetized in the list of works cited under the word or entry that you consulted—not under the title of the reference work itself (see item 13 on p. 139). Either in your text or in your parenthetical reference, mention the word or the entry. No page number is required, since readers can easily look up the word or entry.

The word <u>crocodile</u> has a surprisingly complex etymology ("Crocodile").

13. MULTIVOLUME WORK   If your paper cites more than one volume of a multivolume work, indicate which volume you are referring to, followed by a colon and the page number in the parentheses.

In his studies of gifted children, Terman describes a pattern of

accelerated language acquisition (2: 279).

If your paper cites only one volume of a multivolume work, include the volume number in the list of works cited but not in the parentheses.

14. TWO OR MORE WORKS   To cite more than one source, separate the citations with a semicolon.

The dangers of mountain lions to humans have been well documented

(Rychnovsky 40; Seidensticker 114; Williams 30).

15. AN ENTIRE WORK To cite an entire work, use the author's name in the signal phrase or the parenthetical reference. There is no need to use a page number.

Robinson succinctly describes the status of the mountain lion

controversy in California.

16. WORK IN AN ANTHOLOGY Put the name of the author of the work (not the editor of the anthology) in the signal phrase or the parentheses.

In "A Jury of Her Peers," Mrs. Hale describes both a style of quilting

and a murder weapon when she utters the last words of the story:

"We call it--knot it, Mr. Henderson" (Glaspell 302).

In the list of works cited, the work is alphabetized under Glaspell, not under the name of the editor of the anthology.

17. LEGAL SOURCE For well-known historical documents, such as articles of the United States Constitution, and for laws in the United States Code, provide a parenthetical citation in the text: (US Const., art. 1, sec. 2) or (12 USC 3412, 2000). There is no need to provide a works cited entry.

Legislative acts and court cases are included in the works cited list (see item 50 on p. 147). Your in-text citation should name the act or case either in a signal phrase or in parentheses. In the text of a paper, names of acts are not underlined, but names of cases are.

The Jones Act of 1917 granted U.S. citizenship to Puerto Ricans.

In 1857, Chief Justice Roger B. Taney declared in the case of

Dred Scott v. Sandford that blacks, whether enslaved or free,

could not be citizens of the United States.

Literary works and sacred texts. Literary works and sacred texts are usually available in a variety of editions. When possible, give enough information—such as book parts, play divisions, or line numbers—so that readers can find the cited passage in any edition of the work.

NOTE: The first time you cite a literary work, include the author's name in your citation (as in the examples that follow). You may omit the name in later citations—as long as your context makes clear which work you are citing.

18. LITERARY WORKS WITHOUT PARTS OR LINE NUMBERS When a work has no parts or line numbers, simply cite the page number.

At the end of Kate Chopin's "The Story of an Hour," Mrs. Mallard drops dead upon learning that her husband is alive. In the final irony of the story, doctors report that she has died of a "joy that kills" (25).

19. VERSE PLAYS AND POEMS If possible, give act, scene, and line numbers for verse plays.

In Shakespeare's King Lear, Gloucester, blinded for suspected treason, learns a profound lesson from his tragic experience: "A man may see how this world goes / with no eyes" (4.2.148-49).

For a poem, cite the part and the line numbers, separated by a period.

When Homer's Odysseus comes to the hall of Circe, he finds his men "mild / in her soft spell, fed on her drug of evil" (10.209-11).

For poems that are not divided into parts, use line numbers. For a first reference, use the word "lines": (lines 5–8). Thereafter use just the numbers: (12–13).

20. NOVELS WITH NUMBERED DIVISIONS When a novel has numbered divisions, put the page number first, followed by a semicolon, and then indicate the book, part, or chapter in which the passage may be found. Use abbreviations such as "bk." and "ch."

One of Kingsolver's narrators, teenager Rachel, pushes her vocabulary beyond its limits. For example, Rachel complains that being forced to live in the Congo with her missionary family is "a sheer tapestry of justice" because her chances of finding a boyfriend are "dull and void" (117; bk. 2, ch. 10).

21. SACRED TEXTS When citing a sacred text such as the Bible or the Koran, name the edition in your works cited entry (see item 14, p. 139). In your in-text citation, give the book, chapter, and verse (or their equivalent), separated by periods. Common abbreviations for books of the Bible are acceptable.

Consider the words of Solomon: "If your enemies are hungry, give them food to eat. If they are thirsty, give them water to drink" (Holy Bible, Prov. 25.21).

32b MLA list of works cited

An alphabetized list of works cited, which appears at the end of your research paper, gives publication information for each of the sources you have cited in the paper. (For information about preparing this list, see p. 150; for a sample list of works cited, see p. 152.)

NOTE: Unless your instructor asks for them, omit sources not actually cited in the paper, even if you read them.

General guidelines for listing authors.   Alphabetize entries in the list of works cited by authors' last names (if a work has no author, alphabetize it by its title).

NAME CITED IN TEXT

According to Matt Sundeen, . . .

BEGINNING OF WORKS CITED ENTRY

Sundeen, Matt.

Items 1–5 show how to begin an entry for a work with a single author, multiple authors, a corporate author, an unknown author, and multiple works by the same author. What comes after this first element of your citation will depend on the kind of source you are citing (see items 6–56).

NOTE: For a book, an entry in the works cited list will sometimes begin with an editor (see item 9 on p. 138).

1. SINGLE AUTHOR   Begin the entry with the author's last name, a comma, the author's first name, and a period.

Tannen, Deborah.

2. MULTIPLE AUTHORS   For works with two or more authors, reverse the name of only the first author.

Wilmut, Ian, Keith Campbell, and Colin Tudge.

When a work has four or more authors, either name all of the authors or name the first author, followed by "et al." (Latin for "and others").

Sloan, Frank A., Emily M. Stout, Kathryn Whetten-Goldstein, and
    Lan Liang.

Sloan, Frank A., et al.

3. CORPORATE AUTHOR   When the author of a print document or Web site is a corporation, a government agency, or some other organization, begin with the name of the group.

First Union.

United States. Bureau of the Census.

American Automobile Association.

NOTE: Make sure that your in-text citation also treats the organization as the author (see item 9 on p. 131).

4. UNKNOWN AUTHOR When the author is unknown, begin with the work's title. Titles of articles and other short works, such as brief documents from Web sites, are put in quotation marks. Titles of books and other long works, such as entire Web sites, are underlined.

Article or other short work

"Media Giants."

Book or other long work

Atlas of the World.

5. TWO OR MORE WORKS BY THE SAME AUTHOR If your list of works cited includes two or more works by the same author, use the author's name only for the first entry. For other entries use three hyphens followed by a period. List the titles in alphabetical order.

Atwood, Margaret. Alias Grace: A Novel. New York: Doubleday, 1996.

---, The Robber Bride. New York: Doubleday, 1993.

Books

6. BASIC FORMAT FOR A BOOK For most books, arrange the information into three units, each followed by a period and one space: (1) the author's name; (2) the title and subtitle, underlined; and (3) the place of publication, the publisher, and the date.

```
 ┌──1──┐ ┌────────2────────┐ ┌────────3────────┐
```
Tan, Amy. The Bonesetter's Daughter. New York: Putnam, 2001.

7. AUTHOR WITH AN EDITOR

Kerouac, Jack. Atop an Underwood. Ed. Paul Marion. New York:
    Penguin, 2000.

8. AUTHOR WITH A TRANSLATOR

Allende, Isabel. Daughter of Fortune. Trans. Margaret Sayers Peden.
    New York: Harper, 2000.

9. EDITOR

Craig, Patricia, ed. The Oxford Book of Travel Stories. Oxford: Oxford
    UP, 1996.

10. **WORK IN AN ANTHOLOGY** Begin with (1) the name of the author of the selection. Then give (2) the title of the selection; (3) the title of the anthology; (4) the name of the editor of the anthology (preceded by "Ed." for "Edited by"); (5) publication information; and (6) the pages on which the selection appears.

┌──1──┐ ┌───────2───────┐ ┌─────────3─────────┐
Desai, Anita. "Scholar and Gypsy." The Oxford Book of Travel Stories.

  ┌───4───┐ ┌──────5──────┐ ┌─6─┐
  Ed. Patricia Craig. Oxford: Oxford UP, 1996. 251-73.

11. **EDITION OTHER THAN THE FIRST**
Auletta, Ken. The Underclass. 2nd ed. Woodstock, NY: Overlook, 2000.

12. **MULTIVOLUME WORK**
Conway, Jill Ker, ed. Written by Herself. Vol. 2. New York: Random,
    1996. 2 vols.

13. **ENCYCLOPEDIA OR DICTIONARY ENTRY**
Posner, Rebecca. "Romance Languages." The New Encyclopaedia
    Britannica: Macropaedia. 15th ed. 1987.

"Sonata." The American Heritage Dictionary of the English Language.
    4th ed. 2000.

14. **SACRED TEXT**
Holy Bible: New Living Translation. Wheaton: Tyndale, 1996.

15. **FOREWORD, INTRODUCTION, PREFACE, OR AFTERWORD**
Morris, Jan. Introduction. Letters from the Field, 1925-1975. By
    Margaret Mead. New York: Perennial-Harper, 2001. xix-xxiii.

16. **BOOK WITH A TITLE IN ITS TITLE**
Vanderham, Paul. James Joyce and Censorship: The Trials of Ulysses.
    New York: New York UP, 1997.

Faulkner, Dewey R., ed. Twentieth Century Interpretations of "The
    Pardoner's Tale." Englewood Cliffs: Prentice, 1973.

17. **BOOK IN A SERIES**
Malena, Anne. The Dynamics of Identity in Francophone Caribbean
    Narrative. Francophone Cultures and Lits. Ser. 24. New York:
    Lang, 1998.

18. REPUBLISHED BOOK

Hughes, Langston. <u>Black Misery</u>. 1969. Afterword Robert O'Meally.

    New York: Oxford UP, 2000.

19. PUBLISHER'S IMPRINT

Truan, Barry. <u>Acoustic Communication</u>. Westport: Ablex-Greenwood,

    2000.

Articles in periodicals

This section shows how to prepare works cited entries for articles in magazines, scholarly journals, and newspapers. In addition to consulting the models in this section, you may need to turn to other models as well:

- —More than one author: see item 2 (p. 137)
- —Corporate author: see item 3 (p. 137)
- —Unknown author: see item 4 (p. 138)
- —Article from a subscription service: see item 31 (p. 143)
- —Online article: see item 32 (p. 144)

NOTE: For articles appearing on consecutive pages, provide the page range, such as 121–29 or 298–310. When an article does not appear on consecutive pages, give the number of the first page and a plus sign: 32+.

20. ARTICLE IN A MAGAZINE List (1) the author's name, (2) the title of the article, (3) the title of the magazine, and (4) the date and the page numbers. Abbreviate the names of the months except May, June, and July.

    If the magazine is issued monthly, give just the month and year.

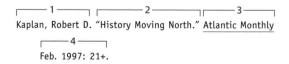

Kaplan, Robert D. "History Moving North." <u>Atlantic Monthly</u>

    Feb. 1997: 21+.

If the magazine is issued weekly, give the exact date.

Lord, Lewis. "There's Something about Mary Todd." <u>US News</u>

    <u>World Report</u> 19 Feb. 2001: 53.

21. ARTICLE IN A JOURNAL PAGINATED BY VOLUME Put the volume number before the year.

Ryan, Katy. "Revolutionary Suicide in Toni Morrison's Fiction." African
American Review 34 (2000): 389-412.

22. ARTICLE IN A JOURNAL PAGINATED BY ISSUE After the volume number, put a period and the issue number.

Wood, Michael. "Broken Dates: Fiction and the Century." Kenyon
Review 22.3 (2000): 50-64.

23. ARTICLE IN A DAILY NEWSPAPER

Murphy, Sean P. "Decisions on Status of Tribes Draw Fire." Boston
Globe 27 Mar. 2001: A2.

Wilford, John Noble. "In a Golden Age of Discovery, Faraway Worlds
Beckon." New York Times 9 Feb. 1997, late ed., sec. 1: 1+.

24. EDITORIAL IN A NEWSPAPER

"All Wet." Editorial. Boston Globe 12 Feb. 2001: A14.

25. LETTER TO THE EDITOR

Moore, Leon. Letter. Chicago Sun-Times 14 Apr. 2003: A11.

26. BOOK OR FILM REVIEW

Gleick, Elizabeth. "The Burdens of Genius." Rev. of The Last Samurai,
by Helen DeWitt. Time 4 Dec. 2000: 171.

Denby, David. "On the Battlefield." Rev. of The Hurricane, dir. Norman
Jewison. New Yorker 10 Jan. 2000: 90-92.

Electronic sources

MLA's guidelines for documenting electronic sources can be found in the *MLA Handbook for Writers of Research Papers* (6th ed., 2003).

NOTE: When a Web address in a works cited entry must be divided at the end of a line, MLA recommends breaking it after a slash. Do not insert a hyphen.

27. AN ENTIRE WEB SITE Begin with (1) the name of the author (if known) and (2) the title of the site. Then give (3) the names of any editors, (4) the date of publication or last update, (5) the name of any sponsoring organization,

(6) the date of access, and (7) the URL. Provide as many of these elements as apply and as are available. For example, in the first model given, items 3 and 5 do not apply.

```
       ┌──── 1 ────┐ ┌──────── 2 ────────┐ ┌─ 4 ─┐ ┌─ 6 ──┐
Peterson, Susan Lynn. The Life of Martin Luther. 1999. 9 Mar. 2001

           ┌─────────────── 7 ───────────────┐
           <http://pweb.netcom.com/~supeters/luther.htm>.
```

United States. Environmental Protection Agency. Values and Functions
    of Wetlands. 25 May 1999. 24 Mar. 2001 <http://
    www.epa.gov-owow/wetlands/facts/fact2.html>.

Margaret Sanger Papers Project. 18 Oct. 2000. History Dept., New York
    U. 3 Apr. 2001 <http://www.nyu.edu/projects/sanger/>.

NOTE: If the site has no title, substitute a description, such as "Home page," for the title.

Block, Marylaine. Home page. 5 Mar. 2001. 12 Apr. 2001 <http://
    www.marylaine.com>.

28. **SHORT WORK FROM A WEB SITE** Short works are those that appear in quotation marks in MLA style: articles and other documents that are not book length. For a short work from a Web site, include as many of the following elements as apply and as are available: (1) author's name, (2) title of the short work, (3) title of the site, (4) date of publication or last update, (5) sponsor of the site (if not named as the author or given as the title), (6) date you accessed the source, and (7) the URL.

Some of these elements may not apply or may be unavailable. In the following example, items 4 and 5 were not available.

```
     ┌── 1 ──┐ ┌──────── 2 ─────────┐ ┌── 3 ──┐
Shiva, Vandana. "Bioethics: A Third World Issue." NativeWeb.

       ┌── 6 ──┐ ┌─────────── 7 ───────────┐
       15 Sept. 2001 <http://www.nativeweb.org/pages/legal/

       shiva.html>.
```

"Media Giants." Frontline: The Merchants of Cool. 2001. PBS Online.
    7 Mar. 2001 <http://www.pbs.org/wgbh/pages/frontline/
    shows/cool/giants>.

NOTE: When the URL for a short work from a Web site is long, you may give the URL for the home page and indicate the path by which readers can access the source.

"Obesity Trends among U.S. Adults between 1985 and 2001." Centers
for Disease Control and Prevention. 3 Jan. 2003. 17 Feb. 2003
<http://www.cdc.gov>. Path: Health Topics A-Z; Obesity Trends;
U.S. Obesity Trends 1985 to 2001.

29. ONLINE BOOK Begin with publication information and end with your date of access and the URL.

Rawlins, Gregory J. E. Moths to the Flame. Cambridge: MIT P, 1996.
3 Apr. 2001 <http://mitpress.mit.edu/e-books/Moths/
contents.html>.

30. PART OF AN ONLINE BOOK

Adams, Henry. "Diplomacy." The Education of Henry Adams. Boston:
Houghton, 1918. Bartleby.com: Great Books Online. 1999.
17 Feb. 2003 <http://bartleby.com/159/8.html>.

31. WORK FROM A SERVICE SUCH AS *INFOTRAC* Libraries pay for access to databases through subscription services such as *InfoTrac.* When you retrieve a work from a subscription service, give as much of the following information as is available: (1) publication information for the source, (2) the name of the database, (3) the name of the service, (4) the name and location of the library where you retrieved the article, (5) your date of access, and (6) the URL of the service.

The following models are for articles retrieved through three popular library subscription services. The *InfoTrac* source is a scholarly article, the *EBSCOhost* source is an article in a magazine, and the *ProQuest* source is an article in a daily newspaper.

Johnson, Kirk. "The Mountain Lions of Michigan." Endangered Species
Update 19.2 (2002): 27+. Expanded Academic Index. InfoTrac.
U of Michigan Lib., Ann Arbor. 26 Nov. 2002 <http://
infotrac.galegroup.com>.

Darnovsky, Marcy. "Embryo Cloning and Beyond." Tikkun July-Aug.
2002: 29-32. Academic Search Premier. EBSCOhost. Portland
Community Coll. Lib., Portland, OR. 1 Nov. 2002 <http://
search.epnet.com>.

Title of article

Headline

Kolata, Gina. "Scientists Debating Future of Hormone Replacement."

New York Times 23 Oct. 2002: A20. ProQuest. Drew U Lib.,

Madison, NJ. 26 Nov. 2002 <http://www.proquest.com>.

NOTE: When you access a work through a personal subscription service such as *America Online,* include the
keyword used to retrieve the source.

Conniff, Richard. "The House That John Built." Smithsonian Feb.

2001. America Online. 11 Mar. 2001. Keyword: Smithsonian

Magazine.

32. **ARTICLE IN AN ONLINE PERIODICAL** When citing online articles, follow the guidelines for printed articles (see items
20–26), giving whatever information is available in the
online source. End the citation with your date of access
and the URL.

NOTE: If the source has numbered paragraphs, include the
total number of paragraphs in your citation.

Belau, Linda. "Trauma and the Material Signifier." Postmodern Culture

11.2 (2001): 37 pars. 30 Mar. 2001 <http://

jefferson.village.virginia.edu/pmc/current.issue/

11.2belau.html>.

Morgan, Fiona. "Banning the Bullies." Salon.com 15 Mar. 2001. 2 Apr.

2001 <http://www.salon.com/news/feature/2001/03/15/

bullying/index.html>.

Whillon, Phil. "Ready or Not." Los Angeles Times 2 Dec. 2001. 3 Dec.

2001 <http://www.latimes.com/news/la-foster-special.special>.

33. **CD-ROM**

"Pimpernel." The American Heritage Dictionary of the English

Language. 4th ed. CD-ROM. Boston: Houghton, 2000.

34. **E-MAIL**

O'Donnell, Patricia. "Re: Interview questions." E-mail to the author.

15 Mar. 2001.

35. **POSTING TO AN ONLINE LIST, FORUM, OR GROUP**

Edwards, David. "Media Lens." Online posting. 20 Dec. 2001. Media

Lens Archives. 10 Apr. 2002 <http://groups.yahoo.com/group/

medialens/message/25>.

Brown, Oliver. "Welcome." Online posting. 8 Oct. 2002. Chester Coll.
    Students Web Forum. 20 Feb. 2003 <http://www.voy.com/
    113243/>.

Reedy, Tom. "Re: Macbeth an Existential Nightmare?" Online posting. 9
    Mar. 2002. 8 Apr. 2002 <news:humanities.lit.authors.shakespe>.

36. POSTING TO A MUD OR A MOO

Carbone, Nick. Planning for the future. 1 Mar. 2001. TechRhet's
    Thursday night MOO. 1 Mar. 2001 <telnet://
    connections.moo.mud.org:3333>.

Multimedia sources (including online versions)

Multimedia sources include visuals, audio works, audio-
visuals, and live events.

When citing multimedia sources that you retrieved
online, consult the appropriate model in this section
and give whatever information is available; then end
the citation with your date of access and the URL. (See
items 37, 40, and 44 for examples.)

37. WORK OF ART

Constable, John. Dedham Vale. Victoria and Albert Museum, London.

van Gogh, Vincent. The Starry Night. 1889. Museum of Mod. Art,
    New York. 3 Feb. 2003 <http://moma.org/collection/depts/
    paint_sculpt/blowups/paint_sculpt_003.html>.

38. CARTOON

Rall, Ted. "Search and Destroy." Cartoon. Village Voice 23 Jan. 2001: 6.

39. ADVERTISEMENT

Truth by Calvin Klein. Advertisement. Vogue Dec. 2000: 95-98.

40. MAP OR CHART

Serbia. Map. 2 Feb. 2001. 17 Mar. 2003 <http://www.biega.com/
    serbia.html>.

Joseph, Lori, and Bob Laird. "Driving While Phoning Is Dangerous."
    Chart. USA Today 16 Feb. 2001: 1A.

41. MUSICAL COMPOSITION

Ellington, Duke. Conga Brava.

Haydn, Franz Joseph. Symphony no. 88 in G.

42. SOUND RECORDING

Bizet, Georges. Carmen. Perf. Jennifer Laramore, Thomas Moser,
  Angela Gheorghiu, and Samuel Ramey. Bavarian State Orch.
  and Chorus. Cond. Giuseppe Sinopoli. Warner, 1996.

Lavigne, Avril. "Complicated." Let Go. Arista, 2002.

43. FILM OR VIDEO

Chocolat. Dir. Lasse Hallström. Perf. Juliette Binoche, Judi
  Dench, Alfred Molina, Lena Olin, and Johnny Depp. Miramax,
  2001.

High Fidelity. Dir. Stephen Frears. Perf. John Cusack, Iben Hjejle,
  Jack Black, and Todd Louiso. 2000. Videocassette. Walt Disney
  Video, 2001.

44. RADIO OR TELEVISION PROGRAM

"Monkey Trial." American Experience. PBS. WGBH, Boston. 18 Mar.
  2003.

"Live in 4A: Konstantin Soukhovetski." Performance Today. Natl.
  Public Radio. 2 May 2002. 10 May 2002 <http://www.npr.org/
  programs/pt/features/4a/soukhovetski.02.html>.

45. RADIO OR TELEVISION INTERVIEW

McGovern, George. Interview. Charlie Rose. PBS. WNET, New York. 1
  Feb. 2001.

46. LIVE PERFORMANCE

Art. By Yasmina Reza. Dir. Matthew Warchus. Perf. Philip Franks,
  Leigh Lawson, and Simon Shephard. Whitehall Theatre, London.
  3 Dec. 2001.

Cello Concerto No. 2. By Eric Tanguy. Cond. Seiji Ozawa. Perf. Mstislav
  Rostropovich. Boston Symphony Orch. Symphony Hall, Boston.
  5 Apr. 2002.

47. LECTURE OR PUBLIC ADDRESS

Cohran, Kelan. "Slavery and Astronomy." Adler Planetarium, Chicago.
  21 Feb. 2001.

48. PERSONAL INTERVIEW

Shaikh, Michael. Personal interview. 22 Mar. 2001.

Other sources (including online versions)

This section includes a variety of traditional print sources not covered elsewhere. For versions obtained on the Web, consult the appropriate model in this section and give whatever information is available; then end the citation with the date of access and the URL. (See the second example under item 49.)

49. GOVERNMENT PUBLICATION

United States. Natl. Council on Disability. Promises to Keep: A Decade
    of Federal Enforcement of the Americans with Disabilities Act.
    Washington: GPO, 2000.

United States. Dept. of Transportation. Natl. Highway Traffic Safety
    Administration. An Investigation of the Safety Implications of
    Wireless Communications in Vehicles. Nov. 1999. 20 May 2001
    <http://www.nhtsa.dot.gov/people/injury/research/wireless>.

50. LEGAL SOURCE For articles of the United States Constitution and laws in the United States Code, no works cited entry is required; instead, simply give an in-text citation (see item 17 on p. 133).

For a legislative act, begin with the name of the act. Then provide the act's Public Law number, its date of enactment, and its Statutes at Large number.

Electronic Freedom of Information Act Amendments of 1996. Pub. L.
    104-418. 2 Oct. 1996. Stat. 3048.

For a court case, name the first plaintiff and first defendant. Then give the case number, the court name, and the date of the decision.

Utah v. Evans. No. 01-714. Supreme Ct. of the US. 20 June 2002.

51. PAMPHLET

Commonwealth of Massachusetts. Dept. of Jury Commissioner. A Few
    Facts about Jury Duty. Boston: Commonwealth of Massachusetts,
    1997.

52. DISSERTATION

Jackson, Shelley. "Writing Whiteness: Contemporary Southern
    Literature in Black and White." Diss. U of Maryland, 2000.

53. ABSTRACT OF A DISSERTATION

Chen, Shu-Ling. "Mothers and Daughters in Morrison, Tan, Marshall, and
    Kincaid." Diss. U of Washington, 2000. DAI 61 (2000): 2289.

54. PUBLISHED PROCEEDINGS OF A CONFERENCE

Kartiganer, Donald M., and Ann J. Abadie. Faulkner at 100: Retrospect
and Prospect. Proc. of Faulkner and Yoknapatawpha Conf., 27 July-
1 Aug. 1997, U of Mississippi. Jackson: UP of Mississippi, 2000.

55. PUBLISHED INTERVIEW

Renoir, Jean. "Renoir at Home: Interview with Jean Renoir." Film
Quarterly 50.1 (1996): 2-8.

56. PERSONAL LETTER

Coggins, Christopher. Letter to the author. 6 May 2001.

32c MLA information notes (optional)

Researchers who use the MLA system of in-text citations (see 32a) may also use information notes for one
of two purposes:

1. to provide additional material that might interrupt
   the flow of the paper yet is important enough to
   include
2. to refer readers to any sources not discussed in the
   paper

Information notes may be footnotes or endnotes.
Footnotes appear at the foot of the page; endnotes appear on a separate page at the end of the paper, just before the list of works cited. For either style, the notes are
numbered consecutively throughout the paper. The text
of the paper contains a raised arabic numeral that corresponds to the number of the note.

TEXT

Local governments are more likely than state governments to pass
legislation against using a cell phone while driving.[1]

NOTE

[1]For a discussion of local laws banning cell phone use, see Sundeen 8.

33 MLA manuscript format; sample pages

33a MLA manuscript format

The following guidelines on formatting a paper and
preparing a list of works cited are consistent with advice
given in the *MLA Handbook for Writers of Research*

Papers, 6th ed. (New York: MLA, 2003). For sample pages from an MLA paper, see 33b.

Formatting the paper. MLA papers should be formatted as follows.

TITLE AND IDENTIFICATION MLA does not require a title page and offers no guidelines for preparing one. On the first page of your paper, place your name, your instructor's name, the course title, and the date on separate lines against the left margin. Then center your title. (See p. 151 for a sample first page.)

If your instructor requires a title page, ask for guidelines on formatting it. A format similar to the one on page 180 will most likely be acceptable.

PAGINATION Put the page number preceded by your last name in the upper right corner of each page, one-half inch below the top edge. Use arabic numerals (1, 2, 3, and so on).

MARGINS, LINE SPACING, AND PARAGRAPH INDENTS Leave margins of one inch on all sides of the page. Do not justify (align) the right margin.

Double-space throughout the paper. Do not add extra lines of space above or below the title of the paper or between paragraphs.

Indent the first line of each paragraph one-half inch (or five spaces) from the left margin.

LONG QUOTATIONS For MLA guidelines on setting off non-fiction quotations, see page 122. For MLA guidelines on setting off literary quotations, see page 126.

WEB ADDRESSES When a Web address mentioned in the text of your paper must be divided at the end of a line, do not insert a hyphen.

HEADINGS MLA neither encourages nor discourages the use of headings and currently provides no guidelines for their use.

VISUALS MLA classifies visuals as tables and figures (figures include graphs, charts, maps, photographs, and drawings). Label each table with an arabic numeral (Table 1, Table 2, and so on) and provide a clear caption that identifies the subject. The label and caption should appear on separate lines above the table, flush left. Below the table, give its source in a note like this one:

Source: John M. Violanti, "Cellular Phones and Fatal Traffic Collisions," Accident Analysis and Prevention 30 (1998): 521.

For each figure, place a label and a caption below the figure, flush left. They need not appear on separate lines. The word "Figure" may be abbreviated to "Fig." Include source information following the caption.

Preparing the list of works cited. Begin the list of works cited on a new page at the end of the paper. Center the title Works Cited about one inch from the top of the page. Double-space throughout. See page 152 for a sample list of works cited.

ALPHABETIZING THE LIST Alphabetize the list by the last names of the authors (or editors); if a work has no author or editor, alphabetize it by the first word of the title other than *A, An,* or *The.*

If your list includes two or more works by the same author, see item 5 on page 138.

INDENTING Do not indent the first line of each works cited entry, but indent any additional lines one-half inch (or five spaces).

WEB ADDRESSES Do not insert a hyphen when dividing a Web address at the end of a line. Break the line after a slash. Also, insert angle brackets around the URL.

If your word processing program automatically turns Web addresses into hot links (by underlining them and highlighting them in color), turn off this feature.

33b Pages from two MLA papers

Following are sample pages from two MLA papers: a research paper written for a composition course and an analysis of a short story written for a literature class.

ON THE WEB | dianahacker.com/pocket

► **Model papers**
  ► MLA papers

Angela Daly
Professor Chavez
English 101
14 March 2001

A Call to Action:

Regulate Use of Cell Phones on the Road

When a cell phone goes off in a classroom or at a concert, we
are irritated, but at least our lives are not endangered. When we are
on the road, however, irresponsible cell phone users are more than
irritating: They are putting our lives at risk. Many of us have
witnessed drivers so distracted by dialing and chatting that they
resemble drunk drivers, weaving between lanes, for example, or nearly
running down pedestrians in crosswalks. A number of bills to regulate
use of cell phones on the road have been introduced in state legisla-
tures, and the time has come to push for their passage. Regulation
is needed because drivers using phones are seriously impaired and
because laws on negligent and reckless driving are not sufficient to
punish offenders.

No one can deny that cell phones have caused traffic deaths
and injuries. Cell phones were implicated in three fatal accidents in
November 1999 alone. Early in November, two-year-old Morgan Pena
was killed by a driver distracted by his cell phone. Morgan's mother,
Patti Pena, reports that the driver "ran a stop sign at 45 mph,
broadsided my vehicle and killed Morgan as she sat in her car seat."
A week later, corrections officer Shannon Smith, who was guarding
prisoners by the side of the road, was killed by a woman distracted
by a phone call (Besthoff). On Thanksgiving weekend that same
month, John and Carole Hall were killed when a Naval Academy
midshipman crashed into their parked car. The driver said in court
that when he looked up from the cell phone he was dialing, he was
three feet from the car and had no time to stop (Stockwell 88).

Expert testimony, public opinion, and even cartoons suggest
that driving while phoning is dangerous. Frances Bents, an expert on
the relation between cell phones and accidents, estimates that
between 450 and 1,000 crashes a year have some connection to cell
phone use (Layton C9). In a survey published by Farmers Insurance

SAMPLE MLA LIST OF WORKS CITED

Works Cited

Besthoff, Len. "Cell Phone Use Increases Risk of Accidents, but Users Willing to Take the Risk." <u>WRAL Online</u>. 11 Nov. 1999. 12 Jan. 2001 <http://www.wral-tv.com/news/wral/1999/1110-talking-driving/>.

Farmers Insurance Group. "New Survey Shows Drivers Have Had 'Close Calls' with Cell Phone Users." <u>Farmers Insurance Group</u>. 8 May 2000. 12 Jan. 2001 <http://www.farmersinsurance.com/news_cellphones.html>.

Haughney, Christine. "Taking Phones out of Drivers' Hands." <u>Washington Post</u> 5 Nov. 2000: A8.

Ippolito, Milo. "Driver's Sentence Not Justice, Mom Says." <u>Atlanta Journal-Constitution</u> 25 Sept. 1999: J1.

Layton, Lyndsey. "Legislators Aiming to Disconnect Motorists." <u>Washington Post</u> 10 Dec. 2000: C1+.

Lowe, Chan. Cartoon. <u>Washington Post</u> 22 July 2000: A21.

Pena, Patricia N. "Patti Pena's Letter to Car Talk." <u>Cars.com</u>. Car Talk. 10 Jan. 2001 <http://cartalk.cars.com/About/Morgan-Pena/letter.html>.

Redelmeier, Donald A., and Robert J. Tibshirani. "Association between Cellular-Telephone Calls and Motor Vehicle Collisions." <u>New England Journal of Medicine</u> 336 (1997): 453-58.

Stockwell, Jamie. "Phone Use Faulted in Collision." <u>Washington Post</u> 6 Dec. 2000: B1+.

Sudeen, Matt. "Cell Phones and Highway Safety: 2000 State Legislative Update." <u>National Conference of State Legislatures</u>. Dec. 2000. 9 pp. 27 Feb. 2001 <http://ncsl.org/programs/esnr/cellphone.pdf>.

Violanti, John M. "Cellular Phones and Fatal Traffic Collisions." <u>Accident Analysis and Prevention</u> 30 (1998): 519-24.

Dan Larson

Professor Duncan

English 102

16 April 2001

The Transformation of Mrs. Peters:

An Analysis of "A Jury of Her Peers"

In Susan Glaspell's 1917 short story "A Jury of Her Peers," two women accompany their husbands and a county attorney to an isolated house where a farmer named John Wright has been choked to death in his bed with a rope. The chief suspect, Wright's wife Minnie, is in jail awaiting trial. The sheriff's wife, Mrs. Peters, has come along to gather some personal items for Minnie, and Mrs. Hale has joined her. Early in the story, Mrs. Hale sympathizes with Minnie and objects to the way the male investigators are "snoopin' round and criticizin'" her kitchen (293). In contrast, Mrs. Peters shows respect for the law, saying that the men are doing "no more than their duty" (293). By the end of the story, however, Mrs. Peters has joined Mrs. Hale in a conspiracy of silence, lied to the men, and committed a crime--hiding key evidence. What causes this dramatic change?

One critic, Leonard Mustazza, argues that Mrs. Hale recruits Mrs. Peters "as a fellow 'juror' in the case, moving the sheriff's wife away from her sympathy for her husband's position and towards identification with the accused woman" (494). While this is true, Mrs. Peters also reaches insights on her own. Her observations in the kitchen lead her to understand Minnie's grim and lonely plight as the wife of an abusive farmer, and her identification with both Minnie and Mrs. Hale is strengthened as the men conducting the investigation trivialize the lives of women.

The first evidence that Mrs. Peters reaches understanding on her own surfaces in the following passage:

> The sheriff's wife had looked from the stove to the sink--to the pail of water which had been carried in from outside. . . . That look of seeing into things, of seeing through a thing to something else, was in the eyes of the sheriff's wife now. (295)

Works Cited

Ben-Zvi, Linda. "'Murder. She Wrote': The Genesis of Susan Glaspell's Trifles." Theatre Journal 44 (1992): 141-62. Rpt. in Susan Glaspell: Essays on Her Theater and Fiction. Ed. Linda Ben-Zvi. Ann Arbor: U of Michigan P. 1995. 19-48.

Glaspell, Susan. "A Jury of Her Peers." Literature and Its Writers: An Introduction to Fiction, Poetry, and Drama. Ed. Ann Charters and Samuel Charters. 2nd ed. Boston: Bedford, 2001. 286-302.

Hedges, Elaine. "Small Things Reconsidered: 'A Jury of Her Peers.'" Women's Studies 12 (1986): 89-110. Rpt. in Susan Glaspell: Essays on Her Theater and Fiction. Ed. Linda Ben-Zvi. Ann Arbor: U of Michigan P. 1995. 49-69.

Mustazza, Leonard. "Generic Translation and Thematic Shift in Susan Glaspell's Trifles and 'A Jury of Her Peers.'" Studies in Short Fiction 26 (1989): 489-96.

Most writing assignments in the social sciences are either reports of original research or reviews of the literature written about a particular research topic. Often an original research report contains a "review of the literature" section that places the writer's project in the context of previous research.

When writing a review of the literature or any other social science paper that draws on written sources, you face three main challenges in addition to documenting those sources: (1) supporting a thesis, (2) avoiding plagiarism, and (3) integrating quotations and other source material. Most social science instructors will ask you to document sources with the American Psychological Association (APA) system described in section 37.

34 Supporting a thesis

A thesis, which usually appears at the end of the introduction, is a one-sentence (or occasionally a two-sentence) statement of your central idea. In a review of the literature paper, this thesis analyzes the often competing conclusions drawn by a variety of researchers.

34a Forming a thesis

You will be reading articles and other sources that address your central research question. Your thesis will express a reasonable answer to that question, given the current state of research in the field. Here, for example, is a research question and a thesis that answers it.

RESEARCH QUESTION

How and to what extent have the great apes -- gorillas, chimpanzees, and orangutans--demonstrated language abilities akin to those of humans?

POSSIBLE THESIS

Researchers agree that apes have acquired fairly large vocabularies in American Sign Language and in artificial languages, but they have drawn quite different conclusions in addressing the following questions: (1) How spontaneously have apes used language? (2) How creatively have apes used language? (3) To what extent can apes create sentences? (4) What are some implications of the ape language studies?

ON THE WEB ⟩ dianahacker.com/pocket

▶ **Electronic research exercises**
   ▶ **APA**
      ▶ Thesis statements in APA papers

34b Organizing your evidence

The American Psychological Association encourages the use of headings to help readers follow the organization of a paper. For an original research report, the major headings often follow a standard model: Method, Results, Discussion. For a paper that reviews the literature on a research topic, headings will vary, depending on the topic. For an example of a heading in an APA paper, see page 181.

---

35 Avoiding plagiarism

Your research paper is a collaboration between you and your sources. To be fair and ethical, you must acknowledge your debt to the writers of those sources. If you don't, you are guilty of plagiarism, a serious academic offense.

Three different acts are considered plagiarism: (1) failing to cite quotations and borrowed ideas, (2) failing to enclose borrowed language in quotation

marks, and (3) failing to put summaries and paraphrases in your own words.

35a Citing quotations and borrowed ideas

You must of course cite all direct quotations or other
material taken directly from a source (for example,
charts or cartoons). You must also cite any ideas borrowed from a source: an author's original insights, any
information summarized or paraphrased from the text,
and statistics and other specific facts.

The only exception is common knowledge—general
information that your readers may know or could easily
locate. For example, the population of the United States
is common knowledge among sociologists, and psychol-
ogists are familiar with Freud's theory of the unconscious. As a rule, when you have seen certain information repeatedly in your reading, you don't need to cite it.
However, when information has appeared in only a few
sources, when it is highly specific (as with statistics), or
when it is controversial, you should cite it.

The American Psychological Association recommends an author-date style of citations. Here, very
briefly, is how the author-date system often works. See
37 for a detailed discussion of variations.

1. The source is introduced by a signal phrase that includes the last names of the authors followed by the
   date of publication in parentheses.
2. The material being cited is followed by a page number in parentheses.
3. At the end of the paper, an alphabetized list of references gives publication information about the
   sources.

IN-TEXT CITATION

Noting that ape's brains resemble those of our human ancestors,
Leakey and Lewin (1992) argued that in ape brains "the cognitive
foundations on which human language could be built are already
present" (p. 244).

ENTRY IN THE LIST OF REFERENCES

Leakey, R., & Lewin, R. (1992). *Origins reconsidered: In search of what
makes us human.* New York: Doubleday.

35b Enclosing borrowed language in quotation marks

To show readers that you are using a source's exact phrases or sentences, you must enclose them in quotation marks. To omit the quotation marks is to claim—falsely—that the language is your own. Such an omission is plagiarism even if you have cited the source.

ORIGINAL SOURCE

No animal has done more to renew interest in animal intelligence than a beguiling, bilingual bonobo named Kanzi, who has the grammatical abilities of a 2-½-year-old child and a taste for movies about cavemen.

—Linden, "Animals," 1986, p. 57

PLAGIARISM

According to Linden (1986), no animal has done more to renew interest in animal intelligence than a beguiling, bilingual bonobo named Kanzi, who has the grammatical abilities of a 2-½-year-old child and a taste for movies about cavemen (p. 57).

BORROWED LANGUAGE IN QUOTATION MARKS

According to Linden (1986), "No animal has done more to renew interest in animal intelligence than a beguiling, bilingual bonobo named Kanzi, who has the grammatical abilities of a 2-½-year-old child and a taste for movies about cavemen" (p. 57).

NOTE: When long quotations are set off from the text by indenting, quotation marks are not needed (see p. 163).

35c Putting summaries and paraphrases in your own words

A summary condenses information; a paraphrase reports information in about the same number of words. When you summarize or paraphrase, you must restate the source's meaning using your own language. You are guilty of plagiarism if you half-copy the author's sentences—either by mixing the author's well-chosen phrases without using quotation marks or by plugging your own synonyms into the author's sentence structure. The following paraphrases are plagiarized—even though the source is cited—because their language is too close to that of the source.

ORIGINAL SOURCE

If the existence of a signing ape was unsettling for linguists, it was also startling news for animal behaviorists.
—Davis, *Eloquent Animals,* 1976, p. 26

UNACCEPTABLE BORROWING OF PHRASES

Davis (1976) observed that the existence of a signing ape unsettled linguists and startled animal behaviorists (p. 26).

UNACCEPTABLE BORROWING OF STRUCTURE

Davis (1976) observed that if the presence of a sign-language using chimp was disturbing for scientists studying language, it was also surprising to scientists studying animal behavior (p. 26).

To avoid plagiarizing an author's language, resist the temptation to look at the source while you are summarizing or paraphrasing—or to download the source and try to change the author's wording. Instead, put the source aside, write from memory or rough notes, and check later for accuracy.

ACCEPTABLE PARAPHRASE

Davis (1976) observed that both linguists and animal behaviorists were taken by surprise upon learning of an ape's ability to use sign language (p. 26).

ON THE WEB | dianahacker.com/pocket

▶ **Electronic research exercises**
  ▶ **APA**
    ▶ Avoiding plagiarism in APA papers

ON THE WEB | dianahacker.com/pocket

▶ **Electronic research exercises**
  ▶ **APA**
    ▶ Recognizing common knowledge in APA papers

36 | Integrating sources

By carefully integrating quotations and other source material into your own text, you help readers understand whose views they are hearing—yours or those of your sources. In addition, you show readers where cited material begins and where it ends.

NOTE: APA recommends using the past tense or the present perfect tense in phrases that introduce most sources: *Davis noted that* or *Davis has noted that* (not *Davis notes that*). Use the present tense, however, for discussing the results of an experiment (*the results show*) or explaining conclusions that are not in dispute (*researchers agree*).

It is generally acceptable in the social sciences to call authors by their last name only, even on a first mention. If your paper refers to two authors with the same last name, use initials as well.

36a Integrating quotations

Readers need to move from your own words to the words of a source without feeling a jolt.

Using signal phrases.   Avoid dropping quotations into the text without warning. Instead, provide clear signal phrases, usually including the author's name and the date of publication, to prepare readers for the quotation.

DROPPED QUOTATION

Perhaps even more significant is the pattern that Kanzi developed on his own in combining various lexigrams. "When he gave an order combining two symbols for action -- such as 'chase' and 'hide' -- it was important for him that the first action -- 'chase' -- be done first" (Gibbons, 1991, p. 1561).

QUOTATION WITH SIGNAL PHRASE

Perhaps even more significant is the pattern that Kanzi developed on his own in combining various lexigrams. According to Gibbons (1991), "When he gave an order combining two symbols for action -- such as 'chase' and 'hide' -- it was important for him that the first action -- 'chase' -- be done first" (p. 1561).

To avoid monotony, try to vary your signal phrases. The following models suggest a range of possibilities.

In the words of Terrace, ". . ."

As Davis has noted, ". . ."

The Gardners, Washoe's trainers, pointed out that ". . ."

". . .," claimed linguist Noam Chomsky.

". . .," wrote Eckholm, ". . ."

Psychologist H. S. Terrace has offered an odd argument for this view: ". . ."

Terrace answered these objections with the following analysis: ". . ."

When the signal phrase includes a verb, choose one that is appropriate in the context. Is your source arguing a point, making an observation, reporting a fact, drawing a conclusion, or refuting an argument? By choosing an appropriate verb, such as one on the following list, you can make your source's stance clear.

admitted	contended	reasoned
agreed	declared	refuted
argued	denied	rejected
asserted	emphasized	reported
believed	insisted	responded
claimed	noted	suggested
compared	observed	thought
confirmed	pointed out	wrote

It is not always necessary to quote full sentences from a source. At times you may wish to borrow only a phrase or to weave part of a source's sentence into your own sentence structure.

Bower (1988) reported that Kanzi practiced "simple grammatical ordering rules," such as putting actions before objects (p. 140).

Using the ellipsis mark.   To condense a quoted passage, you can use the ellipsis mark (three spaced periods) to indicate that you have omitted words. What remains must be grammatically complete.

Eckholm (1985) reported that "a 4-year-old pygmy chimpanzee . . . has demonstrated what scientists say are the most humanlike linguistic skills ever documented in another animal" (p. A1).

The writer has omitted the words *at a research center near Atlanta,* which appeared in the original.

When you want to omit a full sentence or more, use a period before the three ellipsis dots.

According to Wade (1980), the horse Clever Hans "could apparently count by tapping out numbers with his hoof. . . . Clever Hans owes his celebrity to his master's innocence. Von Osten sincerely believed he had taught Hans to solve arithmetical problems" (p. 1349).

Ordinarily, do not use an ellipsis mark at the beginning or at the end of a quotation. Readers will understand that the quoted material is taken from a longer passage. The only exception occurs when you fear that the author's meaning might be misinterpreted without ellipsis marks.

Using brackets.   Brackets (square parentheses) allow you to insert words of your own into quoted material, perhaps to explain a confusing reference or to keep a sentence grammatical in your context.

Seyfarth (1982) has written that "Premack [a scientist at the University of Pennsylvania] taught a seven-year-old chimpanzee, Sarah, that the word for 'apple' was a small, plastic triangle" (p. 13).

To indicate an error in a quotation, insert [*sic*]— italicized and in brackets—after the error.

Setting off long quotations.   When you quote forty or more words, set off the quotation by indenting it one-half inch (or five spaces) from the left margin. Use the normal right margin and do not single-space.

Long quotations should be introduced by an informative sentence, usually followed by a colon. Quotation marks are unnecessary because the indented format tells readers that the words are taken directly from the source.

Hart (1996) has described the kinds of linguistic signs and symbols used in the early ape language experiments:

> Researchers attempted to teach individual signs derived from American Sign Language (ASL) to Washoe, a chimpanzee; Koko, a gorilla; and Chantek, an orangutan. Sarah, a chimpanzee, learned to manipulate arbitrary plastic symbols standing for

words, and another chimpanzee, named Lana, used an early computer keyboard, with arbitrary symbols the researchers called lexigrams. (p. 108)

ON THE WEB > dianahacker.com/pocket

▶ **Electronic research exercises**
   ▶ APA
      ▶ Integrating quotations in APA papers

36b Integrating summaries and paraphrases

Introduce most summaries and paraphrases with a signal phrase that mentions the author and date of publication and places the material in context. Readers will then understand where the summary or paraphrase begins.

Without the signal phrase (underlined) in the following example, readers might think that only the last sentence is being cited, when in fact the whole paragraph is based on the source.

> Studies at the Yerkes Primate Center in Atlanta broke new ground. Researchers Greenfield and Savage-Rumbaugh (1990) reported that the pygmy chimp Kanzi seemed to understand simple grammatical rules about lexigram order. For instance, Kanzi learned that in two-word utterances action precedes object, an ordering also used by human children at the two-word stage. What is impressive, said Greenfield and Savage-Rumbaugh, is that in addition to being semantically related, most of Kanzi's lexigram combinations are original (p. 556).

There are times, however, when a signal phrase naming the author is not necessary. When the context makes clear where the cited material begins, you may omit the signal phrase and include the authors' names in the parentheses: (Greenfield & Savage-Rumbaugh, 1990, p. 556).

36c Integrating statistics and other facts

When you are citing a statistic or other specific fact, a signal phrase is often not necessary. In most cases, readers will understand that the citation refers to the statistic or fact (not the whole paragraph).

By the age of ten, Kanzi had learned to communicate about two hundred symbols on his computerized board (Lewin, 1991, p. 51).

There is nothing wrong, however, with using a signal phrase.

Lewin (1991) reported that by the age of ten Kanzi had learned to communicate about two hundred symbols on his computerized board (p. 51).

37 APA documentation style

To document a source, the American Psychological Association (APA) recommends in-text citations that refer readers to a list of references.

ON THE WEB dianahacker.com/pocket

▶ **Electronic research exercises**
    ▶ APA
        ▶ APA documentation

37a APA in-text citations

The APA's in-text citations provide at least the author's last name and the date of publication. For direct quotations and some summaries and paraphrases, a page number is given as well. In the following models, the elements of the in-text citation are shown in color.

NOTE: APA style requires the use of the past tense or the present perfect tense in signal phrases introducing cited material: *Smith (2003) reported, Smith (2003) has argued.*

1. A QUOTATION   Ordinarily, introduce the quotation with a signal phrase that includes the author's last name followed by the date of publication in parentheses. Put the page number (preceded by "p.") in parentheses after the quotation.

Hart (1996) wrote that some primatologists "wondered if apes had learned Language, with a capital *L*" (p. 109).

If the author is not named in a signal phrase, place the author's last name, the year, and the page number in parentheses after the quotation: (Hart, 1996, p. 109).

2. A SUMMARY OR A PARAPHRASE   Include the author's last name and the date either in a signal phrase introducing the material or in parentheses following it. A page number is not required for a summary or a paraphrase, but include one if it would help readers find the passage in a long work (as in item 3).

According to Hart (1996), researchers took Terrace's conclusions seriously, and funding for language experiments soon declined.

Researchers took Terrace's conclusions seriously, and funding for language experiments soon declined. (Hart, 1996).

3. TWO AUTHORS   Name both authors in the signal phrase or parentheses each time you cite the work. In the parentheses, use "&" between the authors' names; in the signal phrase, use "and."

Greenfield and Savage-Rumbaugh (1990) have acknowledged that Kanzi's linguistic development was slower that that of a human child (p. 567).

Kanzi's linguistic development was slower than that of a human child (Greenfield & Savage-Rumbaugh, 1990, p. 567).

4. THREE TO FIVE AUTHORS Identify all authors in the signal phrase or parentheses the first time you cite the source.

The chimpanzee Nim was raised by researchers who trained him in American Sign Language by molding and guiding his hands (Terrace, Petitto, Sanders, & Bever, 1979).

In subsequent citations, use the first author's name followed by "et al." in either the signal phrase or the parentheses.

Nim was able to string together as many as 16 signs, but their order appeared quite random (Terrace et al., 1979).

5. SIX OR MORE AUTHORS Use the first author's name followed by "et al." in the signal phrase or parentheses.

The ape language studies have shed light on the language development of children with linguistic handicaps (Savage-Rumbaugh et al., 1993).

6. UNKNOWN AUTHOR If the author is unknown, mention the work's title in the signal phrase or give the first word or two of the title in the parenthetical citation. Titles of articles and chapters are put in quotation marks; titles of books and reports are italicized.

A team of researchers in Africa has concluded that many chimpanzee behaviors are cultural, not just responses to environmental factors ("Chimps," 1999).

NOTE: In the rare case when "Anonymous" is specified as the author, treat it as if it were a real name: (Anonymous, 2001). In the list of references, also use the name Anonymous as author.

7. ORGANIZATION AS AUTHOR If the author is a government agency or other organization, name the organization in the signal phrase or the parenthetical citation the first time you cite the source.

According to the Language Research Center (2000), linguistic research with apes has led to new methods of treating humans with learning disabilities such as autism and dyslexia.

If the organization has a familiar abbreviation, you may include it in brackets the first time you cite the source and use the abbreviation alone in later citations.

| First citation | (National Institute of Mental Health [NIMH], 2001) |
| Later citations | (NIMH, 2001) |

8. TWO OR MORE WORKS IN THE SAME PARENTHESES When your parenthetical citation names two or more works, put them in the same order in which they appear in the reference list, separated by semicolons.

Researchers argued that the apes in the early language experiments were merely responding to cues (Sebeok & Umiker-Sebeok, 1979; Terrace, 1979).

9. AUTHORS WITH THE SAME LAST NAME To avoid confusion, use initials with the last names if your reference list includes two or more authors with the same last name.

Research by E. Smith (1989) revealed that . . .

10. PERSONAL COMMUNICATION Cite interviews, letters, e-mail, and other person-to-person communications as follows:

One of Patterson's former aides, who worked with the gorilla Michael, believes that he was capable of joking and lying in sign language (E. Robbins, personal communication, January 4, 2001).

Do not include personal communications in your reference list.

11. AN ELECTRONIC DOCUMENT When possible, cite an electronic document as you would any other document (using the author-date style).

R. Fouts and D. Fouts (1999) have explained one benefit of ape language research: It has shown us how to teach children with linguistic disabilities.

Electronic sources may lack author's names or dates. In addition, they may lack page numbers (required in some citations). Here are APA's guidelines for handling sources without author's names, dates, or page numbers.

Unknown author

If no author is named, mention the title of the document in a signal phrase or give the first word or two of the title in parentheses (see also item 6 on p. 167). (If an organization serves as the author, see item 7 on p. 167.)

According to a BBC article, chimpanzees at sites in West Africa, Tanzania, and Uganda exhibit culture-specific patterns of behavior when grooming one another ("Chimps," 1999).

Unknown date

When the date is unknown, APA recommends using the abbreviation "n.d." (for "no date").

Attempts to return sign-language-using apes to the wild have had mixed results (Smith, n.d.).

No page numbers

APA ordinarily requires page numbers for quotations, and it recommends them for summaries or paraphrases from long sources. When an electronic source lacks stable numbered pages, your citation should include—if possible—information that will help readers locate the particular passage being cited.

When an electronic document has numbered paragraphs, use the paragraph number preceded by the symbol ¶ or by the abbreviation "para.": (Hall, 2001, ¶ 5) *or* (Hall, 2001, para. 5). If neither a page nor a paragraph number is given and the document contains headings, cite the appropriate heading and indicate which paragraph under that heading you are referring to.

According to Kirby (1999), some critics have accused activists in the Great Ape Project of "exaggerating the supposed similarities of the apes [to humans] to stop their use in experiments" (Shared Path section, para. 6).

NOTE: Electronic files using portable document format (PDF) often have stable page numbers. For such sources, give the page number in the parenthetical citation.

12. **INDIRECT SOURCE** If you use a source that was cited in another source (a secondary source), name the original source in your signal phrase. List the secondary source in your reference list and include it in your parenthetical citation, preceded by the words "as cited in." In the following example, Booth is the secondary source.

Linguist Noam Chomsky has dismissed the studies on Kanzi with a flippant analogy: "To maintain that Kanzi has language ability is like saying a man can fly because he can jump in the air" (as cited in Booth, 1990, p. A3).

13. TWO OR MORE WORKS BY THE SAME AUTHOR IN THE SAME YEAR
When your list of references includes more than one
work by the same author in the same year, use lowercase letters ("a," "b," and so on) with the year to order
the entries in the reference list. (See item 6 on p. 172.)
Use those same letters with the year in the in-text
citation.

Research by Kennedy (2000b) has yielded new findings about the role
of gender in the functioning of small groups.

37b APA list of references

In APA style, the alphabetical list of works cited, which
appears at the end of the paper, is titled "References."
Following are models illustrating the form that APA recommends for entries in the list of references. Observe
all details: capitalization, punctuation, italicizing, and
so on. For advice on preparing the references page,
see pages 178–79. For a sample references page, see
page 182.

General guidelines for listing authors

Alphabetize entries in the list of references by authors' last names; if a work has no author, alphabetize it by its title. The first element of each entry is important because citations in the text of the paper refer to it and readers will be looking for it in the alphabetized list. The date of publication appears after the first element of the entry.

NAME AND DATE CITED IN TEXT

Duncan (2003) has reported that . . .

BEGINNING OF ENTRY IN THE LIST OF REFERENCES

Duncan, B. (2003).

Items 1–4 show how to begin an entry for a work with a single author, multiple authors, an organization as author, and an unknown author. Items 5 and 6 show how to begin an entry when your list includes two or more works by the same author or two or more works by the same author in the same year.

What comes after the first element of your citation will depend on the kind of source you are citing (see items 7–31).

1. SINGLE AUTHOR   Begin the entry with the author's last name, followed by a comma and the author's initial(s). Then give the date in parentheses.

Conran, G. (2001).

2. MULTIPLE AUTHORS   List up to six authors by last names, followed by initials. Use an ampersand (&) instead of the word "and."

Walker, J. R., & Taylor, T. (1998).

Sloan, F. A., Stout, E. M., Whetten-Goldstein, K., & Liang, L. (2000).

If there are more than six authors, list the first six and "et al." (meaning "and others").

3. ORGANIZATION AS AUTHOR   When the author is an organization, begin with the name of the organization.

American Psychiatric Association. (2003).

4. UNKNOWN AUTHOR   Begin with the work's title. Titles of books are italicized. Titles of articles are neither italicized nor put in quotation marks.

Oxford essential world atlas. (1996)

EMFs on the brain. (1995, January 21).

5. TWO OR MORE WORKS BY THE SAME AUTHOR   Use the author's name for all entries. List the entries by year, the earliest first.

Schlechty, P. C. (1997).

Schlechty, P. C. (2001).

6. TWO OR MORE WORKS BY THE SAME AUTHOR IN THE SAME YEAR   List the works alphabetically by title. In the parentheses, following the year, add "a," "b," and so on. Use these same letters when giving the year in the in-text citation.

Kennedy, C. (2000a). Group dynamics.

Kennedy, C. (2000b). Share-taking in small groups.

Articles in periodicals

This section shows how to prepare an entry for an article in a journal, a magazine, or a newspaper. You may also need to refer to items 1–6.

NOTE: For articles on consecutive pages, provide the range of pages at the end of the citation (see item 7). When an article does not appear on consecutive pages, give all page numbers (see item 10).

7. ARTICLE IN A JOURNAL PAGINATED BY VOLUME

Morawski, J. (2000). Social psychology a century ago. *American Psychologist, 55,* 427–431.

8. ARTICLE IN A JOURNAL PAGINATED BY ISSUE

Scruton, R. (1996). The eclipse of listening. *The New Criterion, 15*(3), 5–13.

9. ARTICLE IN A MAGAZINE

Shea, R. H. (2002, October 28). E-learning today. *U.S. News & World Report, 133,* 54–56.

10. ARTICLE IN A NEWSPAPER

Haney D. Q. (1998, February 20). Finding eats at mystery of appetite. *The Oregonian,* pp. A1, A17.

11. LETTER TO THE EDITOR

Moller, G. (2002, August). Ripples versus rumbles [Letter to the editor]. *Scientific American, 287* (2), 12.

12. REVIEW

Gleick, E. (2000, December 14). The burdens of genius [Review of the book *The Last Samurai*]. *Time, 156,* 171.

Books

In addition to consulting the items in this section, you may need to refer to items 1–6 on page 172.

13. BASIC FORMAT FOR A BOOK

Highmore, B. (2001). *Everyday life and cultural theory.* New York: Routledge.

14. EDITORS   The first model is for a book with an editor but no author; the second is for a book with an author and an editor. (For a work in an edited book, see item 17.)

Duncan, G. J., & Brooks-Gunn, J. (Eds.). (1997). *Consequences of growing up poor.* New York: Russell Sage Foundation.

Plath, S. (2000). *The unabridged journals* (K. V. Kukil, Ed.). New York: Anchor.

15. TRANSLATION

Singer, I. B. (1998). *Shadows on the Hudson* (J. Sherman, Trans.). New York: Farrar, Straus and Giroux. (Original work published 1957)

16. EDITION OTHER THAN THE FIRST

Helfer, M. E., Keme, R. S., & Drugman, R. D. (1997). *The battered child* (5th ed.). Chicago: University of Chicago Press.

17. ARTICLE OR CHAPTER IN AN EDITED BOOK

Meskell, L. (2001). Archaeologies of identity. In I. Hodder (Ed.), *Archaeological theory today* (pp. 187–213). Cambridge, England: Polity Press.

18. MULTIVOLUME WORK

Wiener, P. (Ed.). (1973). *Dictionary of the history of ideas* (Vols. 1–4). New York: Scribner's.

Electronic sources

19. ARTICLE FROM AN ONLINE PERIODICAL When citing online articles, follow the guidelines for printed articles (see items 7–12), giving whatever information is available in the online source. If the article also appears in a printed journal, a URL is not required; instead, include "Electronic version" in brackets after the title of the article.

Whitmeyer, J. M. (2000). Power through appointment [Electronic version]. *Social Science Research, 29*(4), 535–555.

If there is no print version, include the date you accessed the source and the article's URL.

Ashe, D. D., & McCutcheon, L. E. (2001). Shyness, loneliness, and attitude toward celebrities. *Current Research in Social Psychology, 6*(9). Retrieved July 3, 2001, from http://www.uiowa.edu/~grpproc/crisp/crisp.6.9.htm

20. ARTICLE FROM A DATABASE   To cite an article from an electronic database, include the publication information for the source (see items 7–12). End the citation with your date of access, the name of the database, and the document number (if applicable).

Holliday, R. E., & Hayes, B. K. (2001). Dissociating automatic and
intentional processes in children's eyewitness memory. *Journal
of Experimental Child Psychology, 75*(1), 1–5. Retrieved
February 21, 2001, from Expanded Academic ASAP
database (A59317972).

21. NONPERIODICAL WEB DOCUMENT   To cite a nonperiodical Web document, such as a report, list as many of the following elements as are available: author's name, publication date (or "n.d." if there is no date), title, date of access, and the URL.

Cain, A., & Burris, M. (1999, April). *Investigation of the use of mobile
phones while driving.* Retrieved January 15, 2000, from
http://www.cutr.eng.usf.edu/its/mobile_phone_text.htm

Archer, Z. (n.d.). *Exploring nonverbal communication.* Retrieved July
18, 2001, from http://zzyx.ucsc.edu/~archer

22. CHAPTER OR SECTION IN A WEB DOCUMENT   After the author's name, year, and section title, write "In" and give the title of the document, followed by any identifying information in parentheses. End with your date of access and the URL for the chapter or section.

Heuer, R. J., Jr. (1999). Keeping an open mind. In *Psychology of
intelligence analysis* (chap. 6). Retrieved July 7, 2001, from
http://www.cia.gov/csi/books/19104/art9.html

23. E-MAIL   E-mail messages and other personal communications are not included in the list of references.

24. ONLINE POSTING   If an online posting is not archived, cite it as a personal communication in the text of your paper and do not include it in the list of references. If the posting is archived, treat it as follows, giving as much information as is available.

Eaton, S. (2001, June 12). Online transactions [Msg 2]. Message
posted to news://sci.psychology.psychotherapy.moderated

25. COMPUTER PROGRAM

Ludwig, T. (2002). PsychInquiry [computer software]. New York:
Worth.

Other sources

26. DISSERTATION ABSTRACT

Yoshida, Y. (2001). Essays in urban transportation (Doctoral
dissertation, Boston College, 2001). *Dissertation Abstracts
International, 62,* 7741A.

27. GOVERNMENT DOCUMENT

U.S. Census Bureau. (2000). *Statistical abstract of the United States.*
Washington, DC: U.S. Government Printing Office.

28. REPORT FROM A PRIVATE ORGANIZATION If the publisher is
the author, give the word "Author" as the publisher. If
the report has an author, begin with the author's name,
and name the publisher at the end.

American Psychiatric Association. (2000). *Practice guidelines for
the treatment of patients with eating disorders* (2nd ed.). Washington, DC: Author.

29. CONFERENCE PROCEEDINGS

Schnase, J. L., & Cunnius, E. L. (Eds.). (1995). *Proceedings of CSCL
'95: The First International Conference on Computer Support for
Collaborative Learning.* Mahwah, NJ: Erlbaum.

30. MOTION PICTURE

Soderbergh, S. (Director). (2000). *Traffic* [Motion picture]. United
States: Gramercy Pictures.

31. TELEVISION BROADCAST OR SERIES EPISODE

Pratt, C. (Executive Producer). (2001, December 2). *Face the nation*
[Television broadcast]. Washington, DC: CBS News.

Loeterman, B. (Writer), & Gale, B. (Director). (2000). Real justice
[Television series episode]. In M. Sullivan (Executive Producer),
Frontline. Boston: WGBH.

38 APA manuscript format; sample pages

38a APA manuscript format

The American Psychological Association makes the following recommendations for formatting a paper and preparing a list of references.

Formatting the paper. APA guidelines for formatting a paper are endorsed by many instructors in the social sciences.

TITLE PAGE The APA does not provide guidelines for preparing the title page of a college paper, but instructors may want you to include one. See page 180 for an example.

PAGE NUMBERS AND RUNNING HEAD In the upper right-hand corner of each page, type a short version of your title, followed by five spaces and the page number. Number all pages, including the title page.

MARGINS AND LINE SPACING Use margins of one inch on all sides of the page. Do not justify (align) the right margin. Double-space throughout the paper.

LONG QUOTATIONS See page 163 for APA's guidelines for setting long quotations off from the text.

ABSTRACT If your instructor requires one, include an abstract on its own page after the title page. Center the word Abstract one inch from the top of the page.

An abstract is a 75-to-100-word paragraph that provides readers with a quick overview of your essay. It should express your main idea and your key points; it might also briefly suggest any implications or applications of the research you discuss in the paper.

HEADINGS Although headings are not always necessary, their use is encouraged in the social sciences. For undergraduate papers, one level of heading will usually be sufficient.

In APA style, major headings are centered. Capitalize the first word of the heading, along with all other words except articles, short prepositions, and coordinating conjunctions.

VISUALS The APA classifies visuals as tables and figures (figures include graphs, charts, drawings, and photographs). Keep visuals as simple as possible. Label each table with an arabic numeral (Table 1, Table 2, and so on) and provide a clear title. The label and title should appear on separate lines above the table, flush left. Below the table, give its source in a note:

Note. From "Innovation Roles: From Souls of Fire to Devil's Advocates," by M. Meyer, 2000, *The Journal of Business Communication, 37,* p. 338.

For each figure, place a label and a caption below the figure, flush left. They need not appear on separate lines.

Preparing the list of references. Begin your list of references on a new page at the end of the paper. Center the title References about one inch from the top of the page. Double-space throughout. For a sample reference list, see page 182.

INDENTING ENTRIES APA recommends using a hanging indent: Type the first line of an entry flush left and indent any additional lines one-half inch (or five spaces), as shown in the list on page 182.

ALPHABETIZING THE LIST Alphabetize the reference list by the last names of the authors (or editors); when a work has no author or editor, alphabetize by the first word of the title other than *A, An,* or *The.*

If your list includes two or more works by the same author, arrange the entries by year, the earliest first. If your list includes two or more works by the same author in the same year, arrange them alphabetically by title. Add the letters "a," "b," and so on within the parentheses after the year. Use only the year for journal articles: (2003a). Use the full date for articles in magazines and newspapers in the reference list. Use only the year in all in-text citations.

AUTHORS' NAMES Invert all authors' names and use initials instead of first names. With two or more authors, use an ampersand (&) before the last author's name. Separate the names with commas. Include names for the first six authors; if there are additional authors, end the list with "et al." (Latin for "and others").

TITLES OF BOOKS AND ARTICLES   Italicize the titles and subtitles of books; capitalize only the first word of the title and subtitle (and all proper nouns). Capitalize names of periodicals as you would capitalize them normally (see 89).

ABBREVIATIONS FOR PAGE NUMBERS   Abbreviations for "page" and "pages" ("p." and "pp.") are used before page numbers of newspaper articles and articles in edited books (see item 10 on p. 173 and item 17 on p. 174) but not before page numbers of articles in magazines and journals (see items 7–9 on p. 173).

BREAKING A URL   When a URL must be divided, break it after a slash or before a period. Do not insert a hyphen.

38b Sample APA pages

Following are sample pages from a "review of the literature" research paper written for a psychology class.

ON THE WEB   dianahacker.com/pocket

▶   **Model papers**
   ▶   APA paper

Apes and Language:

A Review of the Literature

Karen Shaw

Psychology 110, Section 2

Professor Verdi

April 5, 2001

Apes and Language

A Review of the Literature

Over the past 30 years, researchers have demonstrated that the great apes (chimpanzees, gorillas, and orangutans) resemble humans in language abilities more than had been thought possible. Just how far that resemblance extends, however, has been a matter of some controversy. Researchers agree that the apes have acquired fairly large vocabularies in American Sign Language and in artificial languages, but they have drawn quite different conclusions in addressing the following questions:

1. How spontaneously have apes used language?

2. How creatively have apes used language?

3. Can apes create sentences?

4. What are the implications of the ape language studies?

This review of the literature on apes and language focuses on these four questions.

How Spontaneously Have Apes Used Language?

In an influential article, Terrace, Petitto, Sanders, and Bever (1979) argued that the apes in language experiments were not using language spontaneously but were merely imitating their trainers, responding to conscious or unconscious cues. Terrace and his colleagues at Columbia University had trained a chimpanzee, Nim, in American Sign Language, so their skepticism about the apes' abilities received much attention. In fact, funding for ape language research was sharply reduced following publication of their 1979 article "Can an Ape Create a Sentence?"

In retrospect, the conclusions of Terrace et al. seem to have been premature. Although some early ape language studies had not been rigorously controlled to eliminate cuing, even as early as the 1970s R. A. Gardner and B. T. Gardner were conducting double-blind experiments that prevented any possibility of cuing (Fouts, 1997, p. 99). Since 1979, researchers have diligently guarded against cuing.

Perhaps the best evidence that apes are not merely responding to

SAMPLE APA LIST OF REFERENCES

References

Begley S. (1998, January 19). Aping language. *Newsweek, 131,* 56-58.

Booth, W. (1990, October 29) Monkeying with language: Is chimp using words or merely aping handlers? *The Washington Post,* p. A3.

Eckholm, E. (1985, June 25). Kanzi the chimp: A life in science. *The New York Times,* pp. C1, C3.

Fouts, R. (1997). *Next of kin: What chimpanzees have taught me about who we are.* New York: William Morrow.

Gibbons, A. (1991). Déjà vu all over again: Chimp-language wars. *Science, 251,* 1561-1562.

Greenfield, P. M., & Savage-Rumbaugh, E. S. (1990). Grammatical combination in *Pan paniscus:* Processes of learning and invention in the evolution and development of language. In S. T. Parker & K. R. Gibson (Eds.), *"Language" and intelligence in monkeys and apes: Comparative developmental perspectives* (pp. 540-578). Cambridge: Cambridge University Press.

Leakey, R., & Lewin, R. (1992). *Origins reconsidered: In search of what makes us human.* New York: Doubleday.

O'Sullivan, C., & Yeager, C. P. (1989). Communicative context and linguistic competence: The effect of social setting on a chimpanzee's conversational skill. In R. A. Garner, B. T. Gardner, & T. E. Van Cantfort (Eds.), *Teaching sign language to chimpanzees* (pp. 269-279). Albany: SUNY Press.

Patterson, F., & Linden, E. (1981). *The education of Koko.* New York: Holt, Rinehart & Winston.

Rumbaugh, D. (1995). Primate language and cognition: Common ground. *Social Research, 62,* 711-730.

Most assignments in history and other humanities classes are based to some extent on reading. At times you will be asked to respond to one or two readings, such as essays or historical documents. At other times you may be asked to write a research paper that draws on a wide variety of sources.

Most history instructors and some humanities instructors require the *Chicago*-style footnotes or endnotes explained in section 42. When you write a paper that draws on written sources, you face three main challenges in addition to documenting those sources: (1) supporting a thesis, (2) avoiding plagiarism, and (3) integrating quotations and other source material.

39   Supporting a thesis

Most assignments ask you to form a thesis, or main idea, and to support that thesis with well-organized evidence.

39a   Forming a thesis

A thesis is a one-sentence (or occasionally a two-sentence) statement of your central idea. Usually your thesis will appear at the end of the first paragraph (as in the example on p. 206), but if you need to provide readers with considerable background information, you may place it in the second paragraph.

The thesis of your paper will be a reasoned answer to the central research question you pose, as in the following example.

RESEARCH QUESTION

To what extent was Confederate Major General Nathan Bedford Forrest responsible for the massacre of Union troops at Fort Pillow?

POSSIBLE THESIS

Although we will never know whether Nathan Bedford Forrest directly ordered the massacre of Union troops at Fort Pillow, evidence suggests that he was responsible for it.

Notice that the thesis expresses a view on a debatable issue — an issue about which intelligent, well-meaning people might disagree. The writer's job is to convince such readers that this view is worth taking seriously.

ON THE WEB dianahacker.com/pocket

▶ **Electronic research exercises**
  ▶ *Chicago*
    ▶ Thesis statements in *Chicago* papers

39b Organizing your evidence

The body of your paper will consist of evidence in support of your thesis. Instead of getting tangled up in a complex, formal outline, sketch an informal plan that organizes your evidence in bold strokes. The student who wrote about Fort Pillow used a simple list of questions as the blueprint for his paper. In the paper itself, these became headings that helped readers follow the writer's line of argument.

> What happened at Fort Pillow?
>
> Did Forrest order the massacre?
>
> Can Forrest be held responsible for the massacre?

---

40 Avoiding plagiarism

Your research paper is a collaboration between you and your sources. To be fair and ethical, you must acknowledge your debt to the writers of those sources. If you don't, you are guilty of plagiarism, a serious academic offense.

Three different acts are considered plagiarism: (1) failing to cite quotations and borrowed ideas, (2) failing to enclose borrowed language in quotation marks, and (3) failing to put summaries and paraphrases in your own words.

40a Citing quotations and borrowed ideas

You must of course cite all direct quotations or other material taken directly from a source (for example, charts or cartoons). You must also cite any ideas borrowed from a source: an author's original insights, any information summarized or paraphrased from the text, and statistics and other specific facts.

The only exception is common knowledge—general information that your readers may know or could easily locate. For example, the population of the United States is common knowledge among sociologists and economists, and historians are familiar with facts such as the date of the Emancipation Proclamation. As a rule, when you have seen certain general information repeatedly in your reading, you don't need to cite it. However, when information has appeared in only a few sources, when it is highly specific (as with statistics), or when it is controversial, you should cite it.

Chicago citations consist of numbered notes in the text of the paper that refer readers to notes with corresponding numbers either at the foot of the page (footnotes) or at the end of the paper (endnotes).

TEXT

Governor John Andrew was not allowed to recruit black soldiers from out of state. "Ostensibly," writes Peter Burchard, "no recruiting was done outside Massachusetts, but it was an open secret that Andrew's agents were working far and wide."[1]

NOTE

1. Peter Burchard, *One Gallant Rush: Robert Gould Shaw and His Brave Black Regiment* (New York: St. Martin's, 1965), 85.

For detailed advice on using *Chicago* notes, see 42a. When you use footnotes or endnotes, you will usually need to provide a bibliography as well (see 42b).

40b Enclosing borrowed language in quotation marks

To show readers that you are using a source's exact phrases or sentences, you must enclose them in quotation marks. To omit the quotation marks is to claim—falsely—that the language is your own. Such an omission is plagiarism even if you have cited your source.

ORIGINAL SOURCE

For many Southerners it was psychologically impossible to see a black man bearing arms as anything but an incipient slave uprising complete with arson, murder, pillage, and rapine.

> —Dudley Taylor Cornish, *The Sable Arm: Negro Troops in the Union Army, 1861–1865,* p. 158

PLAGIARISM

According to Civil War historian Dudley Taylor Cornish, for many Southerners it was psychologically impossible to see a black man bearing arms as anything but an incipient slave uprising complete with arson, murder, pillage, and rapine.[2]

BORROWED LANGUAGE IN QUOTATION MARKS

According to Civil War historian Dudley Taylor Cornish, "For many Southerners it was psychologically impossible to see a black man bearing arms as anything but an incipient slave uprising complete with arson, murder, pillage, and rapine."[2]

NOTE: When quoted sentences are set off from the text by indenting, quotation marks are not needed (see p. 192).

40c Putting summaries and paraphrases in your own words

A summary condenses information; a paraphrase reports information in about the same number of words. When you summarize or paraphrase, you must restate the source's meaning using your own language.

In the following example, the paraphrase is plagiarized—even though the source is cited—because too much of its language is borrowed from the source without quotation marks. The underlined phrases have been copied word-for-word. In addition, the writer has closely followed the sentence structure of the original source, merely plugging in some synonyms (such as *fifty percent* for *half* and *savage hatred* for *fierce, bitter animosity*).

ORIGINAL SOURCE

Half of the force holding Fort Pillow were Negroes, former slaves now enrolled in the Union Army. Toward them Forrest's troops had the fierce, bitter animosity of men who had been educated to regard the colored race as inferior and who for the first time had encountered that race armed and fighting against white men. The sight enraged and perhaps terrified many of the Confederates and aroused in them the ugly spirit of a lynching mob.
　　　　　—Albert Castel, "The Fort Pillow Massacre,"
　　　　　pp. 46–47

PLAGIARISM: UNACCEPTABLE BORROWING

Albert Castel suggests that much of the brutality at Fort Pillow can be traced to racial attitudes. Fifty percent of the troops holding Fort Pillow were Negroes, former slaves who had joined the Union Army. Toward them Forrest's soldiers displayed the savage hatred of men who had been taught the inferiority of blacks and who for the first time had confronted them armed and fighting against white men. The vision angered and perhaps frightened the Confederates and aroused in them the ugly spirit of a lynching mob.[3]

To avoid plagiarizing an author's language, resist the temptation to look at the source while you are summarizing or paraphrasing—or to download the source and try to change the author's wording. Instead, put the source aside, write from memory or rough notes, and check later for accuracy.

ACCEPTABLE PARAPHRASE

Albert Castel suggests that much of the brutality at Fort Pillow can be traced to racial attitudes. Nearly half of the Union troops were blacks, men whom the Confederates had been raised to consider their inferiors. The shock and perhaps fear of facing armed ex-slaves in battle for the first time may well have unleashed the fury that led to the massacre.[3]

| ON THE WEB | dianahacker.com/pocket |

▶ **Electronic research exercises**
   ▶ *Chicago*
      ▶ Avoiding plagiarism in *Chicago* papers

| ON THE WEB | dianahacker.com/pocket |

▶ **Electronic research exercises**
   ▶ *Chicago*
      ▶ Recognizing common knowledge in *Chicago* papers

41   Integrating sources

By carefully integrating quotations and other source material into your own text, you help readers understand whose views they are hearing—yours or those of your sources. In addition, you show readers where cited material begins (your note shows where it ends).

NOTE: As a rule, use the present tense or present perfect tense in phrases that introduce quotations or other source materials: *Foote points out that* or *Foote has pointed out that* (not *Foote pointed out that*). If you have good reason to emphasize that the author's language or opinion was articulated in the past, however, the past tense is acceptable.

The first time you mention an author, use the full name: *Shelby Foote argues. . . .* When you refer to the author again, you may use the last name only: *Foote raises an important question.*

41a   Integrating quotations

Readers should be able to move from your own words to the words you quote from a source without feeling a jolt.

Using signal phrases.   Avoid dropping quotations into the text without warning. Instead, provide clear signal phrases, usually including the author's name, to prepare readers for the source.

DROPPED QUOTATION

Those testifying on the Union and Confederate sides recalled events at Fort Pillow quite differently. Unionists claimed that their troops had abandoned their arms and were in full retreat. "The Confederates, however, all agreed that the Union troops retreated to the river with arms in their hands."[4]

QUOTATION WITH SIGNAL PHRASE

Those testifying on the Union and Confederate sides recalled events at Fort Pillow quite differently. Unionists claimed that their troops had abandoned their arms and were in full retreat. "The Confederates, however," writes historian Albert Castel, "all agreed that the Union troops retreated to the river with arms in their hands."[4]

To avoid monotony, try to vary your signal phrases. The following models suggest a range of possibilities.

> In the words of historian James M. McPherson, ". . ."
>
> As Dudley Taylor Cornish has argued, ". . ."
>
> In a letter to his wife, a Confederate soldier who witnessed the massacre wrote that ". . ."
>
> ". . . ," claims Benjamin Quarles.
>
> ". . . ," notes Albert Castel, ". . ."
>
> Shelby Foote offers an intriguing interpretation of these events: ". . ."

When the signal phrase includes a verb, choose one that is appropriate in the context. Is your source arguing a point, making an observation, reporting a fact, refuting an argument, or stating a belief? By choosing an appropriate verb, such as one on the following list, you can make your source's stance clear.

admits	compares	insists	rejects
agrees	confirms	notes	reports
argues	contends	observes	responds
asserts	declares	points out	suggests
believes	denies	reasons	thinks
claims	emphasizes	refutes	writes

It is not always necessary to quote full sentences from a source. At times you may wish to borrow only a phrase or to weave part of a source's sentence into your own sentence structure.

As Hurst has pointed out, until there was "an outcry in the northern press," even the Confederates did not deny that there had been a massacre at Fort Pillow.[5]

Using the ellipsis mark.   To condense a quoted passage, you can use the ellipsis mark (three spaced periods) to indicate that you have omitted words. The sentence that remains must be grammatically complete.

Union surgeon Fitch's testimony that all women and children had been evacuated from Fort Pillow before the attack conflicts with Forrest's report: "We captured . . . about 40 negro women and children."[7]

The writer has omitted several words not relevant to the issue at hand: *164 Federals, 75 negro troops, and.*

When you want to omit a full sentence or more, use a period before the three ellipsis dots. For an example, see the long quotation on page 192.

Ordinarily, do not use an ellipsis mark at the beginning or at the end of a quotation. Readers will understand that the quoted material is taken from a longer passage.

Using brackets.   Brackets allow you to insert words of your own into quoted material, perhaps to explain a confusing reference or to keep a sentence grammatical in your context.

According to Albert Castel, "It can be reasonably argued that he [Forrest] was justified in believing that the approaching steamships intended to aid the garrison [at Fort Pillow]."[8]

NOTE: Use [*sic*] to indicate that an error in a quoted sentence appears in the original source. (An example appears in the long quotation on p. 192.) However, if a source is filled with errors, as is the case with many historical documents, this use of [*sic*] can become distracting and is best avoided.

Setting off long quotations.   *Chicago* style allows you some leeway in deciding whether to set off a quotation or run it into your text. For emphasis you may want to set off a quotation of more than four or five lines of text; almost certainly you should set off quotations of eight lines or more. To set off a quotation, indent it one-half inch (or five spaces) from the left margin and use the normal right margin. Double-space the indented quotation.

Long quotations should be introduced by an informative sentence, usually followed by a colon. Quotation marks are unnecessary because the indented format tells readers that the words are taken directly from the source.

In a letter home, Confederate officer Achilles V. Clark recounted what happened at Fort Pillow:

> Words cannot describe the scene. The poor deluded negroes
> would run up to our men fall upon their knees and with
> uplifted hands scream for mercy but they were ordered to their
> feet and then shot down. The whitte [*sic*] men fared but little
> better. . . . I with several others tried to stop the butchery and
> at one time had partially succeeded, but Gen. Forrest ordered
> them shot down like dogs, and the carnage continued.[9]

ON THE WEB   dianahacker.com/pocket

▶ **Electronic research exercises**
   ▶ *Chicago*
      ▶ Integrating quotations in *Chicago* papers

41b Integrating summaries and paraphrases

Summaries and paraphrases are written in your own words. As with quotations, you should introduce most summaries and paraphrases with a signal phrase that names the author and places the material in context. Readers will then understand that everything between the signal phrase and the numbered note summarizes or paraphrases the cited source.

Without the signal phrase (underlined) in the following example, readers might think that only the last sentence is being cited, when in fact the whole paragraph is based on the source.

<u>According to Kenneth Davis</u>, official Confederate policy was that
black soldiers were to be treated as runaway slaves; in addition, the
Confederate Congress decreed that white Union officers commanding
black troops be killed. Confederate Lieutenant General Kirby Smith of

Mississippi boldly announced that he would kill all captured black troops. Smith's policy never met with strong opposition from the Richmond government.[10]

When the context makes clear where the cited material begins, however, you may omit the signal phrase.

41c Integrating statistics and other facts

When you are citing a statistic or other specific fact, a signal phrase is often not necessary. In most cases, readers will understand that the citation refers to the statistic or fact (not the whole paragraph).

Of the 295 white troops garrisoned at Fort Pillow, 168 were taken prisoner. Black troops fared much worse, with only 58 of 262 men being taken into custody.[11]

There is nothing wrong, however, with using a signal phrase.

Shelby Foote notes that of the 295 white troops garrisoned at Fort Pillow, 168 were taken prisoner but that black troops fared much worse, with only 58 of 262 men being taken into custody.[11]

42 *Chicago* documentation style (footnotes or endnotes)

Professors in history and some humanities often require footnotes or endnotes based on *The Chicago Manual of Style,* 15th ed. (Chicago: U of Chicago P, 2003). When you use *Chicago*-style notes, you will usually be asked to include a bibliography at the end of your paper. (See 42b.)

ON THE WEB	dianahacker.com/pocket

► **Electronic research exercises**
  ► *Chicago*
    ► *Chicago* documentation

42a First and subsequent references to a source

The first time you cite a source, the note should include publishing information for that work as well as the page number on which the specific quotation, paraphrase, or summary may be found.

1. Peter Burchard, *One Gallant Rush: Robert Gould Shaw and His Brave Black Regiment* (New York: St. Martin's, 1965), 85.

For subsequent references to a source you have already cited, you may simply give the author's last name, a short form of the title, and the page or pages cited. A short form of the title of a book is italicized; a short form of the title of an article is put in quotation marks.

4. Burchard, *One Gallant Rush,* 31.

When you have two consecutive notes from the same source, you may use "Ibid." (meaning "in the same place") and the page number for the second note. Use "Ibid." alone if the page number is the same.

5. Jack Hurst, *Nathan Bedford Forrest: A Biography* (New York: Knopf, 1993), 8.

6. Ibid., 174.

42b *Chicago*-style bibliography

A bibliography, which appears at the end of your paper, lists every work you have cited in your notes; in addition, it may include works that you consulted but did not cite. For advice on constructing the list, see page 203. A sample bibliography appears on page 208.

NOTE: If you include a bibliography, *The Chicago Manual of Style* suggests that you shorten all notes, including the first reference to a source, as described in 42a. Check with your instructor, however, to see whether using an abbreviated note for a first reference to a source is acceptable.

42c Model notes and bibliographic entries

The following models are consistent with guidelines set forth in *The Chicago Manual of Style,* 15th ed. For each type of source, a model note appears first, followed by a model bibliographic entry. The model note shows the format you should use when citing a source for the first time. For subsequent citations of a source, use shortened notes (see 42a).

DIRECTORY TO *CHICAGO*-STYLE NOTES AND BIBLIOGRAPHIC ENTRIES

Books (print and online)

1. **BASIC FORMAT FOR A PRINT BOOK**

   1. William H. Rehnquist, *The Supreme Court: A History* (New York: Knopf, 2001), 204

   Rehnquist, William H. *The Supreme Court: A History.* New York: Knopf, 2001.

2. **BASIC FORMAT FOR AN ONLINE BOOK**

   2. Heinz Kramer, *A Changing Turkey: The Challenge to Europe and the United States* (Washington, DC: Brookings Press, 2000), 85, http://brookings.nap.edu/books/0815750234/html/index.html.

   Kramer, Heinz. *A Changing Turkey: The Challenge to Europe and the United States.* Washington, DC: Brookings Press, 2000. http://brookings.nap.edu/books/0815750234/html/index.html.

3. **TWO OR THREE AUTHORS**

   3. Michael D. Coe and Mark Van Stone, *Reading the Maya Glyphs* (London: Thames & Hudson, 2002), 129-30.

   Coe, Michael D., and Mark Van Stone. *Reading the Maya Glyphs.* London: Thames & Hudson, 2002.

4. **FOUR OR MORE AUTHORS**

   4. Lynn Hunt and others, *The Making of the West: Peoples and Cultures* (Boston: Bedford, 2001), 541.

   Hunt, Lynn, Thomas R. Martin, Barbara H. Rosenwein, R. Po-chia Hsia, and Bonnie G. Smith. *The Making of the West: Peoples and Cultures.* Boston: Bedford, 2001.

5. **UNKNOWN AUTHOR**

   5. *The Men's League Handbook on Women's Suffrage* (London, 1912), 23.

   The Men's League Handbook on Women's Suffrage. London, 1912.

6. **EDITED WORK WITHOUT AN AUTHOR**

   6. Jack Beatty, ed., *Colossus: How the Corporation Changed America* (New York: Broadway Books, 2001), 127.

   Beatty, Jack, ed. *Colossus: How the Corporation Changed America.* New York: Broadway Books, 2001.

7. **EDITED WORK WITH AN AUTHOR**

   7. Ted Poston, *A First Draft of History,* ed. Kathleen A. Hauke (Athens: University of Georgia Press, 2000), 46.

Poston, Ted. *A First Draft of History*. Edited by Kathleen A. Hauke. Athens: University of Georgia Press, 2000.

8. TRANSLATED WORK

8. Tonino Guerra, *Abandoned Places,* trans. Adria Bernardi (Barcelona: Guernica, 1999), 71.

Guerra, Tonino. *Abandoned Places*. Translated by Adria Bernardi. Barcelona: Guernica, 1999.

9. EDITION OTHER THAN THE FIRST

9. Andrew F. Rolle, *California: A History,* 5th ed. (Wheeling, IL: Harlan Davidson, 1998), 243.

Rolle, Andrew F. *California: A History*. 5th ed. Wheeling, IL: Harlan Davidson, 1998.

10. VOLUME IN A MULTIVOLUME WORK

10. James M. McPherson, *Ordeal by Fire,* vol. 2, *The Civil War* (New York: McGraw-Hill, 1993), 205.

McPherson, James M. *Ordeal by Fire.* Vol. 2, *The Civil War*. New York: McGraw-Hill, 1993.

11. WORK IN AN ANTHOLOGY

11. Zora Neale Hurston, "From *Dust Tracks on a Road,*" in *The Norton Book of American Autobiography,* ed. Jay Parini (New York: Norton, 1999), 336.

Hurston, Zora Neale. "From *Dust Tracks on a Road*." In *The Norton Book of American Autobiography,* edited by Jay Parini, 333-43. New York: Norton, 1999.

12. LETTER IN A PUBLISHED COLLECTION

12. Thomas Gainsborough to Elizabeth Rasse, 1753, in *The Letters of Thomas Gainsborough,* ed. John Hayes (New Haven: Yale University Press, 2001), 5.

Gainsborough, Thomas. Letter to Elizabeth Rasse, 1753. In *The Letters of Thomas Gainsborough,* edited by John Hayes, 5. New Haven: Yale University Press, 2001.

13. WORK IN A SERIES

13. R. Keith Schoppa, *The Columbia Guide to Modern Chinese History,* Columbia Guides to Asian History (New York: Columbia University Press, 2000), 256-58.

Schoppa, R. Keith. *The Columbia Guide to Modern Chinese History*. Columbia Guides to Asian History. New York: Columbia University Press, 2000.

14. **ENCYCLOPEDIA OR DICTIONARY**

14. *Encyclopaedia Britannica,* 15th ed., s.v. "Monroe Doctrine."

NOTE: The abbreviation "s.v." is for the Latin *sub verbo* ("under the word").

Reference works are usually not included in the bibliography.

15. **SACRED TEXT**

15. Matt. 20.4-9 (Revised Standard Version).

The Bible is usually not included in the bibliography.

Articles in periodicals (print and online)

16. **ARTICLE IN A JOURNAL** For an article in a print journal, include the volume and issue numbers and the date; end the bibliography entry with the page range of the article.

16. Jonathon Zimmerman, "Ethnicity and the History Wars in the 1920s," *Journal of American History* 87, no. 1 (2000): 101.

Zimmerman, Jonathon. "Ethnicity and the History Wars in the 1920s." *Journal of American History* 87, no. 1 (2000): 92-111.

For an article accessed through a database service such as *EBSCOhost* or for an article published online, include a URL. If the article is paginated, give a page number in the note and a page range in the bibliography. For unpaginated articles, page references are not possible, but in your note you may include a "locator," such as a numbered paragraph or a heading from the article, as in the example for an article published online.

Journal article from a database service

16. Eugene F. Provenzo Jr., "Time Exposure," *Educational Studies* 34, no. 2 (2003): 266, http://search.epnet.com.

Provenzo, Eugene F. Jr. "Time Exposure." *Educational Studies* 34, no. 2 (2003): 266-67. http://search.epnet.com.

Journal article published online

16. Linda Belau, "Trauma and the Material Signifier," *Postmodern Culture* 11, no. 2 (2001): par. 6, http://www.iath.virginia.edu/pmc/text-only/issue.101/11.2belau.txt.

Belau, Linda. "Trauma and the Material Signifier." *Postmodern Culture* 11, no. 2 (2001). http://www.iath.virginia.edu/pmc/text-only/issue.101/11.2belau.txt.

17. ARTICLE IN A MAGAZINE For a print article, provide a page number in the note and a page range in the bibliography.

> 17. Joy Williams, "One Acre," *Harper's,* February 2001, 62.

Williams, Joy. "One Acre." *Harper's,* February 2001, 58-65.

For an article accessed through a database service such as *FirstSearch* or for an article published online, include a URL. If the article is paginated, give a page number in the note and a page range in the bibliography. For unpaginated articles, page references are not possible.

Magazine article from a database service

> 17. David Pryce-Jones, "The Great Sorting Out: Postwar Iraq," *National Review*, May 5, 2003, 17, http://newfirstsearch.oclc.org.

Pryce-Jones, David. "The Great Sorting Out: Postwar Iraq." *National Review*, May 5, 2003, 17-18. http://newfirstsearch.oclc.org.

Magazine article published online

> 17. Fiona Morgan, "Banning the Bullies," *Salon*, March 15, 2001, http://www.salon.com/news/feature/2001/03/15/bullying/index.html.

Morgan, Fiona. "Banning the Bullies." *Salon*, March 15, 2001. http://www.salon.com/news/feature/2001/03/15/bullying/index.html.

18. ARTICLE IN A NEWSPAPER For newspaper articles—whether in print or online—page numbers are not necessary. A section letter or number, if available, is sufficient.

> 18. Dan Barry, "A Mill Closes, and a Hamlet Fades to Black," *New York Times,* February 16, 2001, sec. A.

Barry, Dan. "A Mill Closes, and a Hamlet Fades to Black." *New York Times,* February 16, 2001, sec. A.

For an article accessed through a database such as *ProQuest* or for an article published online, include a URL.

Newspaper article from a database service

> 18. Gina Kolata, "Scientists Debating Future of Hormone Replacement," *New York Times*, October 23, 2002, http://www.proquest.com.

Kolata, Gina. "Scientists Debating Future of Hormone Replacement." *New York Times*, October 23, 2002. http://www.proquest.com.

Newspaper article published online

18. Phil Willon, "Ready or Not," *Los Angeles Times*, December 2, 2001, http://www.latimes.com/news/la-foster-special.special.

Willon, Phil. "Ready or Not." *Los Angeles Times*, December 2, 2001. http://www.latimes.com/news/la-foster-special.special.

19. UNSIGNED ARTICLE When the author of a periodical is unknown, treat the periodical itself as the author.

19. *Boston Globe*, "Renewable Energy Rules," August 11, 2003, sec. A.

Boston Globe. "Renewable Energy Rules." August 11, 2003, sec. A.

20. BOOK REVIEW

20. Nancy Gabin, review of *The Other Feminists: Activists in the Liberal Establishment,* by Susan M. Hartman, *Journal of Women's History* 12, no. 3 (2000): 230.

Gabin, Nancy. Review of *The Other Feminists: Activists in the Liberal Establishment,* by Susan M. Hartman. *Journal of Women's History* 12, no. 3 (2000): 227-34.

Web sites and postings

21. WEB SITE Include as much of the following information as is available: author, title of the site, sponsor of the site, and the site's URL. When no author is named, treat the sponsor as the author.

21. Kevin Rayburn, *The 1920s,* http://www.louisville.edu/~kprayb01/1920s.html.

Rayburn, Kevin. *The 1920s.* http://www.louisville.edu/~kprayb01/1920s.html.

NOTE: *The Chicago Manual of Style* does not advise including the date you accessed a Web source, but you may provide an access date after the URL if the cited material is time-sensitive: for example, dianahacker.com/pocket (accessed June 3, 2003).

22. SHORT DOCUMENT FROM A WEB SITE Include as many of the following elements as are available: author's name, title of the short work, title of the site, sponsor of the site, and the URL. When no author is named, treat the site's sponsor as the author.

22. Sheila Connor, "Historical Background," *Garden and Forest,* Library of Congress, http://lcweb.loc.gov/preserv/prd/gardfor/historygf.html.

Connor, Sheila. "Historical Background." *Garden and Forest.* Library of
   Congress. http://lcweb.loc.gov/preserv/prd/gardfor/
   historygf.html.

22. PBS Online, "Media Giants," *Frontline: The Merchants of Cool,*
http://www.pbs.org/wgbh/pages/frontline/shows/cool/giants.

PBS Online. "Media Giants." *Frontline: The Merchants of Cool.*
   http://www.pbs.org/wgbh/pages/frontline/shows/cool/giants.

23. ONLINE POSTING OR E-MAIL   If an online posting has been
archived, include a URL, as in the following example.
E-mails that are not part of an online discussion are
treated as personal communications (see item 26).
Online postings and e-mails are not included in the bibliography.

23. Janice Klein, posting to State Museum Association discussion
list, June 19, 2003, http://listserv.nmmnh-abq.mus.nm.us/scripts/
wa.exe?A2=ind0306c&L=sma-l&F=lf&S=&P=81.

Other sources (print, online, multimedia)

24. GOVERNMENT DOCUMENT
   24. U.S. Department of State, *Foreign Relations of the United
States: Diplomatic Papers,* 1943 (Washington, DC: GPO, 1965), 562.

U.S. Department of State. *Foreign Relations of the United States:
   Diplomatic Papers,* 1943. Washington, DC: GPO, 1965.

25. UNPUBLISHED DISSERTATION
   25. Stephanie Lynn Budin, "The Origins of Aphrodite (Greece)"
(PhD diss., University of Pennsylvania, 2000), 301-2.

Budin, Stephanie Lynn. "The Origins of Aphrodite (Greece)." PhD
   diss., University of Pennsylvania, 2000.

26. PERSONAL COMMUNICATION
   26. Sara Lehman, e-mail to author, August 13, 2003.

Personal communications are not included in the bibliography.

27. PUBLISHED OR BROADCAST INTERVIEW
   27. Ron Haviv, interview by Charlie Rose, *The Charlie Rose
Show,* Public Broadcasting System, February 12, 2001.

Haviv, Ron. Interview by Charlie Rose. *The Charlie Rose Show.* Public
   Broadcasting System, February 12, 2001.

28. VIDEO OR DVD

28. *The Secret of Roan Inish,* DVD, directed by John Sayles (1993; Culver City, CA: Columbia Tristar Home Video, 2000).

The Secret of Roan Inish. DVD. Directed by John Sayles. 1993; Culver City, CA: Columbia Tristar Home Video, 2000.

29. SOUND RECORDING

29. Gustav Holst, *The Planets,* Royal Philharmonic, André Previn, Telarc compact disc 80133.

Holst, Gustav. *The Planets.* Royal Philharmonic. André Previn. Telarc compact disc 80133.

30. SOURCE QUOTED IN ANOTHER SOURCE

30. Adam Smith, *The Wealth of Nations* (New York: Random House, 1965), 11, quoted in Mark Skousen, *The Making of Modern Economics: The Lives and the Ideas of the Great Thinkers* (Armonk, NY: M. E. Sharpe, 2001), 15.

Smith, Adam. *The Wealth of Nations,* 11. New York: Random House, 1965. Quoted in Mark Skousen, *The Making of Modern Economics: The Lives and the Ideas of the Great Thinkers* (Armonk, NY: M. E. Sharpe, 2001), 15.

43 *Chicago* manuscript format; sample pages

43a *Chicago* manuscript format

The following guidelines for formatting a *Chicago* paper and preparing its endnotes and bibliography are based on *The Chicago Manual of Style,* 15th ed. For pages from a sample paper, see 43b.

Formatting the paper. *Chicago* manuscript guidelines are fairly generic, since they were not created with a specific type of writing in mind.

TITLE PAGE Include the full title of your paper, your name, the course title, the instructor's name, and the date. Do not number the title page but count it in the manuscript numbering; that is, the first page of the text will be numbered 2. See page 205 for a sample title page.

PAGINATION   Using arabic numerals, number all pages except the title page in the upper right corner. You may place your last name to the left of the page number if you wish.

MARGINS AND LINE SPACING   Leave margins of at least one inch at the top, bottom, and sides of the page. Double-space the text of the manuscript, including long quotations that have been set off from the text. (For line spacing in notes and the bibliography, see below and p. 204.)

LONG QUOTATIONS   See page 191 for *Chicago* guidelines for setting long quotations off from the text.

Preparing the endnotes.   Begin the endnotes on a new page at the end of the paper. Center the title Notes about one inch from the top of the page, and number the pages consecutively with the rest of the manuscript. See page 207 for an example.

INDENTING AND NUMBERING   Indent the first line of each entry one-half inch (or five spaces) from the left margin; do not indent additional lines in an entry. Begin the note with the arabic numeral that corresponds to the numbered note in the text. Put a period after the number.

LINE SPACING   Single-space each note and double-space between notes (unless your instructor prefers double-spacing throughout).

Preparing the bibliography.   Typically, the notes in *Chicago* papers are followed by a bibliography, an alphabetically arranged list of all the works cited or consulted (see p. 208 for an example). Center the title Bibliography about one inch from the top of the page. Number bibliography pages consecutively with the rest of the paper.

ALPHABETIZING THE LIST   Alphabetize the bibliography by the last names of the authors (or editors); when a work has no author or editor, alphabetize by the first word of the title other than *A, An,* or *The.*

   If your list includes two or more works by the same author, use three hyphens instead of the author's name in all entries after the first. You may arrange the entries alphabetically by title or chronologically; be consistent throughout the bibliography.

INDENTING AND LINE SPACING   Begin each entry at the left margin, and indent any additional lines one-half inch (or five spaces). Single-space each entry and double-space between entries (unless your instructor prefers double-spacing throughout).

43b   Sample pages from a *Chicago* paper

Following are sample pages from a research paper written for a history class.

ON THE WEB   dianahacker.com/pocket
► **Model papers**
  ► *Chicago* paper

The Massacre at Fort Pillow:

Holding Nathan Bedford Forrest Accountable

Ned Bishop

History 214

Professor Citro

March 22, 1999

Although Northern newspapers of the time no doubt exaggerated some of the Confederate atrocities at Fort Pillow, most modern sources agree that a massacre of Union troops took place there on April 12, 1864. It seems clear that Union soldiers, particularly black soldiers, were killed after they had stopped fighting or had surrendered or were being held prisoner. Less clear is the role played by Confederate Major General Nathan Bedford Forrest in leading his troops. Although we will never know whether Forrest directly ordered the massacre, evidence suggests that he was responsible for it.

What happened at Fort Pillow?

Fort Pillow, Tennessee, which sat on a bluff overlooking the Mississippi River, had been held by the Union for two years. It was garrisoned by 580 men, 292 of them from the Sixth United States Colored Heavy and Light Cavalry, 285 from the white Thirteenth Tennessee Cavalry. Nathan Bedford Forrest's troops numbered about 1,500 men.[1]

The Confederates attacked Fort Pillow on April 12, 1864, and had virtually surrounded the fort by the time Forrest arrived on the battlefield. At 3:30 P.M., Forrest displayed a flag of truce and sent in a demand for unconditional surrender of the sort he had used before: "The conduct of the officers and men garrisoning Fort Pillow has been such as to entitle them to being treated as prisoners of war. . . . Should my demand be refused, I cannot be responsible for the fate of your command."[2] Union Major William Bradford, who had replaced Major Booth, killed earlier by sharpshooters, asked for an hour to consult. Forrest, worried that vessels in the river were bringing more troops, shortened the time to twenty minutes. Bradford refused to surrender, and Forrest quickly ordered the attack.

The Confederates charged across the short distance between their lines and the fort, helping one another scale the parapet, from which they fired into the fort. Victory came quickly, with the Union forces running toward the river or surrendering. Shelby Foote describes the scene like this:

> Some kept going, right into the river, where a number drowned and the swimmers became targets for marksmen on the bluff.

Notes

1. John Cimprich and Robert C. Mainfort Jr., "Fort Pillow Revisited: New Evidence about an Old Controversy," *Civil War History* 28, no. 4 (1982): 293-94.

2. Brian Steel Wills, *A Battle from the Start: The Life of Nathan Bedford Forrest* (New York: HarperCollins, 1992), 182.

3. Shelby Foote, *The Civil War, a Narrative: Red River to Appomattox* (New York: Vintage, 1986), 110.

4. Nathan Bedford Forrest, "Report of Maj. Gen. Nathan Bedford Forrest, C. S. Army, Commanding Cavalry, of the Capture of Fort Pillow," *Shotgun's Home of the American Civil War,* http://www.civilwarhome.com/forrest.htm.

5. Jack Hurst, *Nathan Bedford Forrest: A Biography* (New York: Knopf, 1993), 174.

6. Foote, *Civil War,* 111.

7. Cimprich and Mainfort, "Fort Pillow," 305.

8. Ibid., 299.

9. Foote, *Civil War,* 110.

10. Wills, *Battle from the Start,* 187.

11. Albert Castel, "The Fort Pillow Massacre: A Fresh Examination of the Evidence," *Civil War History* 4, no. 1 (1958): 44-45.

12. Cimprich and Mainfort, "Fort Pillow," 300.

13. Hurst, *Nathan Bedford Forrest,* 177.

14. Ibid.

15. Dudley Taylor Cornish, *The Sable Arm: Black Troops in the Union Army, 1861-1865* (Lawrence, KS: University Press of Kansas, 1987), 175.

16. Foote, *Civil War,* 111.

17. Cimprich and Mainfort, "Fort Pillow," 304.

18. Wills, *Battle from the Start,* 189.

Bibliography

Castel, Albert. "The Fort Pillow Massacre: A Fresh Examination of the Evidence." *Civil War History* 4, no. 1 (1958): 37-50.

Cimprich, John, and Robert C. Mainfort Jr. "Fort Pillow Revisited: New Evidence about an Old Controversy." *Civil War History* 28, no. 4 (1982): 293-306.

Cornish, Dudley Taylor. *The Sable Arm: Black Troops in the Union Army, 1861-1865.* Lawrence, KS: University Press of Kansas, 1987.

Foote, Shelby. *The Civil War, a Narrative: Red River to Appomattox.* New York: Vintage, 1986.

Forrest, Nathan Bedford. "Report of Maj. Gen. Nathan Bedford Forrest, C. S. Army, Commanding Cavalry, of the Capture of Fort Pillow." *Shotgun's Home of the American Civil War.* http://www.civilwarhome.com/forrest.htm.

Hurst, Jack. *Nathan Bedford Forrest: A Biography.* New York: Knopf, 1993.

McPherson, James M. *Battle Cry of Freedom: The Civil War Era.* New York: Oxford University Press, 1988.

Wills, Brian Steel. *A Battle from the Start: The Life of Nathan Bedford Forrest.* New York: HarperCollins, 1992.

This glossary includes words commonly confused, words commonly misused, and words that are nonstandard. It also lists colloquialisms that may be appropriate in informal speech but are often considered inappropriate in formal writing.

a, an Use *an* before a vowel sound, *a* before a consonant sound: *an apple, a peach.* Problems sometimes arise with words beginning with *h.* If the *h* is silent, the word begins with a vowel sound, so use *an: an hour, an heir, an honest senator, an honorable deed.* If the *h* is pronounced, the word begins with a consonant sound, so use *a: a hospital, a hymn, a historian, a hotel.* When an abbreviation or acronym begins with a vowel sound, use *an: an EKG, an MRI, an AIDS patient.*

accept, except *Accept* is a verb meaning "to receive." *Except* is usually a preposition meaning "excluding." *I will accept all the packages except that one. Except* is also a verb meaning "to exclude." *Please except that item from the list.*

adapt, adopt *Adapt* means "to adjust or become accustomed"; it is usually followed by *to. Adopt* means "to take as one's own." *Our family adopted a Vietnamese orphan, who quickly adapted to his new surroundings.*

adverse, averse *Adverse* means "unfavorable." *Averse* means "opposed" or "reluctant"; it is usually followed by *to. I am averse to your proposal because it could have an adverse impact on the economy.*

advice, advise *Advice* is a noun, *advise* a verb. *We advise you to follow John's advice.*

affect, effect *Affect* is usually a verb meaning "to influence." *Effect* is usually a noun meaning "result." *The drug did not affect the disease, and it had several adverse side effects. Effect* can also be a verb meaning "to bring about." *Only the president can effect such a dramatic change.*

all ready, already *All ready* means "completely prepared." *Already* means "previously." *Susan was all ready for the concert, but her friends had already left.*

all right *All right* is correct. *Alright* is nonstandard.

all together, altogether *All together* means "everyone gathered." *Altogether* means "entirely." *We were not altogether certain that we could bring the family all together for the reunion.*

allusion, illusion An *allusion* is an indirect reference; an *illusion* is a misconception or false impression. *Did you catch my allusion to Shakespeare? Mirrors give the room an illusion of depth.*

a lot *A lot* is two words. Do not write *alot*.

among, between Ordinarily, use *among* with three or more entities, *between* with two. *The prize was divided among several contestants. You have a choice between carrots and beans.*

amoral, immoral *Amoral* means "neither moral nor immoral"; it also means "not caring about moral judgments." *Immoral* means "morally wrong." *Until recently, most business courses were taught from an amoral perspective. Murder is immoral.*

amount, number Use *amount* with quantities that cannot be counted; use *number* with those that can. *This recipe calls for a large amount of sugar. We have a large number of toads in our garden.*

an See *a, an*.

and/or Avoid *and/or* except in technical or legal documents.

anxious *Anxious* means "worried" or "apprehensive." In formal writing, avoid using *anxious* to mean "eager." *We are eager* (not *anxious*) *to see your new house.*

anybody, anyone See pages 25–26 and 37.

anyone, any one *Anyone,* an indefinite pronoun, means "any person at all." *Any one* refers to a particular person or thing in a group. *Anyone from Chicago may choose any one of the games on display.*

anyways, anywheres *Anyways* and *anywheres* are nonstandard for *anyway* and *anywhere*.

as *As* is sometimes used to mean "because." But do not use it if there is any chance of ambiguity. *We canceled the picnic because* (not *as*) *it began raining.* An *as* here could mean "because" or "when."

as, like See *like, as*.

averse See *adverse, averse*.

awful The adjective *awful* means "awe-inspiring." Colloquially it is used to mean "terrible" or "bad." The adverb *awfully* is sometimes used in conversation as an intensifier meaning "very." In formal writing, avoid these colloquial uses. *I was very* (not *awfully*) *upset last night.*

awhile, a while *Awhile* is an adverb; it can modify a verb, but it cannot be the object of a preposition such as *for*. The two-word form *a while* is a noun preceded by an article and therefore can be the object of a preposition. *Stay awhile. Stay for a while.*

back up, backup   *Back up* is a verb phrase. *Back up the car carefully. Be sure to back up your hard drive.* A *backup* is a duplicate of electronically stored data. *Keep your backup in a safe place. Backup* can also be used as an adjective. *I regularly create backup disks.*

bad, badly   *Bad* is an adjective, *badly* an adverb. *They felt bad about being early and ruining the surprise. Her arm hurt badly after she slid into second.* See section 13.

being as, being that   *Being as* and *being that* are nonstandard expressions. Write *because* or *since* instead.

beside, besides   *Beside* is a preposition meaning "at the side of" or "next to." *Annie Oakley slept with her gun beside her bed. Besides* is a preposition meaning "except" or "in addition to." *No one besides Terrie can have that ice cream. Besides* is also an adverb meaning "in addition." *I'm not hungry; besides, I don't like ice cream.*

between   See *among, between.*

bring, take   Use *bring* when an object is being transported toward you, *take* when it is being moved away. *Please bring me a glass of water. Please take these magazines to Mr. Scott.*

can, may   *Can* is traditionally reserved for ability, *may* for permission. *Can you ski down the advanced slope without falling? May I help you?*

capital, capitol   *Capital* refers to a city, *capitol* to a building where lawmakers meet. *The residents of the state capital protested the development plans. The capitol has undergone extensive renovations. Capital* also refers to wealth or resources.

censor, censure   *Censor* means "to remove or suppress material considered objectionable." *Censure* means "to criticize severely." *The school's policy of censoring books has been censured by the media.*

cite, site   *Cite* means "to quote as an authority or example." *Site* is usually a noun meaning "a particular place." *He cited the zoning law in his argument against the proposed site of the gas station.* Locations on the Internet are usually referred to as *sites. The library's Web site improves every week.*

coarse, course   *Coarse* means "crude" or "rough in texture." *The coarse weave of the wall hanging gave it a three-dimensional quality. Course* usually refers to a path, a playing field, or a unit of study; the expression *of course* means "certainly." *I plan to take a course in car repair this summer. Of course, you are welcome to join me.*

complement, compliment *Complement* is a verb meaning "to go with or complete" or a noun meaning "something that completes." *Compliment* as a verb means "to flatter"; as a noun it means "flattering remark." *Her skill at rushing the net complements his skill at volleying. Sheiying's music arrangements receive many compliments.*

conscience, conscious *Conscience* is a noun meaning "moral principles"; *conscious* is an adjective meaning "aware or alert." *Let your conscience be your guide. Were you conscious of his love for you?*

continual, continuous *Continual* means "repeated regularly and frequently." *She grew weary of the continual telephone calls. Continuous* means "extended or prolonged without interruption." *The broken siren made a continuous wail.*

could care less *Could care less* is a nonstandard expression. Write *couldn't care less* instead.

could of *Could of* is nonstandard for *could have.*

council, counsel A *council* is a deliberative body, and a *councilor* is a member of such a body. *Counsel* usually means "advice" and can also mean "lawyer"; *counselor* is one who gives advice or guidance. *The councilors met to draft the council's position paper. The pastor offered wise counsel to the troubled teenager.*

criteria *Criteria* is the plural of *criterion,* which means "a standard, rule, or test on which a judgment or decision can be based." *The only criterion for the job is a willingness to work overtime.*

data Although technically plural, *data* is now accepted as a singular noun. *The new data suggest* (or *suggests*) *that our theory is correct.* (The singular *datum* is rarely used.)

different from, different than Ordinarily, write *different from. Your sense of style is different from Jim's.* However, *different than* is acceptable to avoid an awkward construction. *Please let me know if your plans are different than* (to avoid *from what*) *they were six weeks ago.*

don't *Don't* is the contraction for *do not. I don't want any. Don't* should not be used as the contraction for *does not,* which is *doesn't. He doesn't* (not *don't*) *want any.*

due to *Due to* is an adjective phrase and should not be used as a preposition meaning "because of." *The trip was canceled because of* (not *due to*) *lack of interest. Due to* is acceptable as a subject complement and usually follows a form of the verb *be. His success was due to hard work.*

each See pages 25–26 and 37.

effect See *affect, effect.*

either See pages 25–26 and 37.

elicit, illicit *Elicit* is a verb meaning "to bring out" or "to evoke." *Illicit* is an adjective meaning "unlawful." *The reporter was unable to elicit any information from the police about illicit drug traffic.*

emigrate from, immigrate to *Emigrate* means "to leave one country or region to settle in another." *In 1900, my grandfather emigrated from Russia to escape the religious pogroms. Immigrate* means "to enter another country and reside there." *Many Mexicans immigrate to the United States to find work.*

enthused As an adjective, *enthusiastic* is preferred. *The children were enthusiastic* (not *enthused*) *about going to the circus.*

etc. Avoid ending a list with *etc.* It is more emphatic to end with an example, and in most contexts readers will understand that the list is not exhaustive. When you don't wish to end with an example, *and so on* is more graceful than *etc.*

everybody, everyone See pages 25–26 and 37.

everyone, every one *Everyone* is an indefinite pronoun. *Everyone wanted to go. Every one,* the pronoun *one* preceded by the adjective *every,* means "each individual or thing in a particular group." *Every one* is usually followed by *of. Every one of the missing books was found.*

except See *accept, except.*

farther, further *Farther* describes distances. *Detroit is farther from Miami than I thought. Further* suggests quantity or degree. *You extended the curfew further than you should have.*

fewer, less *Fewer* refers to items that can be counted; *less* refers to general amounts. *Fewer people are living in the city. Please put less sugar in my tea.*

firstly *Firstly* sounds pretentious, and it leads to the ungainly series *firstly, secondly, thirdly, fourthly,* and so on. Write *first, second, third* instead.

further See *farther, further.*

good, well See page 45.

graduate Both of the following uses of *graduate* are standard: *My sister was graduated from UCLA last year. My sister graduated from UCLA last year.* It is nonstandard, however, to drop the word *from: My sister graduated UCLA last year.* Though this usage is common in informal English, many readers object to it.

grow Phrases such as *to grow the economy* and *to grow a business* are jargon. Usually the verb *grow* is intransitive (it does not take a direct object). *Our business has grown very quickly.* When *grow* is used in a transitive sense, with a direct object, it means "to cultivate" or "to allow to grow." *We plan to grow tomatoes this year. John is growing a beard.*

hanged, hung *Hanged* is the past-tense and past-participle form of the verb *hang,* meaning "to execute." *The prisoner was hanged at dawn.* *Hung* is the past-tense and past-participle form of the verb *hang,* meaning "to fasten or suspend." *The stockings were hung by the chimney with care.*

hardly Avoid expressions such as *can't hardly* and *not hardly,* which are considered double negatives. *I can* (not *can't*) *hardly describe my elation at getting the job.*

he At one time *he* was used to mean "he or she." Today such usage is inappropriate. See pages 21 and 37 for alternative constructions.

hisself *Hisself* is nonstandard. Use *himself.*

hopefully *Hopefully* means "in a hopeful manner." *We looked hopefully to the future.* Some usage experts object to the use of *hopefully* as a sentence adverb, apparently on grounds of clarity. To be safe, avoid using *hopefully* in sentences such as the following: *Hopefully, your son will recover soon.* At least some educated readers will want you to indicate who is doing the hoping: *I hope that your son will recover soon.*

however In the past, some writers objected to *however* at the beginning of a sentence, but current experts advise you to place the word according to your meaning and desired emphasis. Any of the following sentences is correct, depending on the intended contrast. *Pam decided, however, to attend Harvard. However, Pam decided to attend Harvard.* (She had been considering other schools.) *Pam, however, decided to attend Harvard.* (Unlike someone else, Pam opted for Harvard.)

hung See *hanged, hung.*

illusion See *allusion, illusion.*

imply, infer *Imply* means "to suggest or state indirectly"; *infer* means "to draw a conclusion." *John implied that he knew all about computers, but the interviewer inferred that John was inexperienced.*

ingenious, ingenuous *Ingenious* means "clever." *Sarah's solution to the problem was ingenious.* *Ingenuous* means "naive" or "frank." *For a successful manager, Ed is surprisingly ingenuous.*

in, into *In* indicates location or condition; *into* indicates movement or a change in condition. *They found the lost letters in a box after moving into the house.*

in regards to *In regards to* confuses two different phrases: *in regard to* and *as regards*. Use one or the other. *In regard to* (or *As regards*) *the contract, ignore the first clause.*

irregardless *Irregardless* is nonstandard. Use *regardless*.

is when, is where See section 6c.

its, it's *Its* is a possessive pronoun; *it's* is a contraction for *it is. The dog licked its wound whenever its owner walked into the room. It's a perfect day to walk the twenty-mile trail.*

kind of, sort of Avoid using *kind of* or *sort of* to mean "somewhat." *The movie was a little* (not *kind of*) *boring.* Do not put *a* after either phrase. *That kind of* (not *kind of a*) *salesclerk annoys me.*

lay, lie See page 30.

lead, led *Lead* is a noun referring to a metal. *Led* is the past tense of the verb *to lead. He led me to the treasure.*

learn, teach *Learn* means "to gain knowledge"; *teach* means "to impart knowledge." *I must teach* (not *learn*) *my sister to read.*

leave, let Avoid the nonstandard use of *leave* ("to exit") to mean *let* ("to permit"). *Let* (not *Leave*) *me help you with the dishes.*

less See *fewer, less*.

let, leave See *leave, let*.

liable *Liable* means "obligated" or "responsible." Do not use it to mean "likely." *You're likely* (not *liable*) *to trip if you don't tie your shoelaces.*

lie, lay See page 30.

like, as *Like* is a preposition, not a subordinating conjunction. It should be followed only by a noun or a noun phrase. *As* is a subordinating conjection that introduces a subordinate clause. In casual speech you may say *She looks like she hasn't slept* or *You don't know her like I do.* But in formal writing, use *as. She looks as if she hasn't slept. You don't know her as I do.*

loose, lose *Loose* is an adjective meaning "not securely fastened." *Lose* is a verb meaning "to misplace" or "to not win." *Did you lose your only loose pair of work pants?*

may See *can, may*.

maybe, may be *Maybe* is an adverb meaning "possibly"; *may be* is a verb phrase. *Maybe the sun will shine tomorrow. Tomorrow may be a brighter day.*

may of, might of *May of* and *might of* are nonstandard for *may have* and *might have.*

media, medium *Media* is the plural of *medium. Of all the media that cover the Olympics, television is the medium that best captures the spectacle of the events.*

must of See *may of.*

myself *Myself* is a reflexive or intensive pronoun. Reflexive: *I cut myself.* Intensive: *I will drive you myself.* Do not use *myself* in place of *I* or *me: He gave the plants to Melinda and me* (not *myself*).

neither See pages 25–26 and 37.

none See pages 25–26 and 37.

nowheres *Nowheres* is nonstandard for *nowhere.*

number See *amount, number.*

off of *Off* is sufficient. Omit *of.*

passed, past *Passed* is the past tense of the verb *to pass. Emily passed me another slice of cake. Past* usually means "belonging to a former time" or "beyond a time or place." *Our past president spoke until past midnight. The hotel is just past the next intersection.*

plus *Plus* should not be used to join independent clauses. *This raincoat is dirty; moreover* (not *plus*), *it has a hole in it.*

precede, proceed *Precede* means "to come before." *Proceed* means "to go forward." *As we proceeded up the mountain, we noticed fresh tracks in the mud, evidence that a group of hikers had preceded us.*

principal, principle *Principal* is a noun meaning "the head of a school or organization" or "a sum of money." It is also an adjective meaning "most important." *Principle* is a noun meaning "a basic truth or law." *The principal expelled her for three principal reasons. We believe in the principle of equal justice for all.*

proceed, precede See *precede, proceed.*

quote, quotation *Quote* is a verb; *quotation* is a noun. Avoid using *quote* as a shortened form of the noun. *Her quotations* (not *quotes*) *from the Upanishads intrigued us.*

real, really *Real* is an adjective; *really* is an adverb. *Real* is sometimes used informally as an adverb, but avoid this use in formal writing. *She was really* (not *real*) *angry.* (See section 13.)

reason . . . is because   See section 6c.

reason why   The expression *reason why* is redundant. *The reason* (not *The reason why*) *Jones lost the election is clear.*

respectfully, respectively   *Respectfully* means "showing or marked by respect." *He respectfully submitted his opinion to the judge. Respectively* means "each in the order given." *John, Tom, and Larry were a butcher, a baker, and a lawyer, respectively.*

sensual, sensuous   *Sensual* means "gratifying the physical senses," especially those associated with sexual pleasure. *Sensuous* means "pleasing to the senses," especially those involved in the experience of art, music, and nature. *The sensuous music and balmy air led the dancers to more sensual movements.*

set, sit   *Set* means "to put" or "to place"; *sit* means "to be seated." *She set the dough in a warm corner of the kitchen. The cat sits in the warmest part of the room.*

should of   *Should of* is nonstandard for *should have.*

since   Do not use *since* to mean "because" if there is any chance of ambiguity. *Because* (not *Since*) *we won the game, we have been celebrating with a pitcher of beer. Since* here could mean "because" or "from the time that."

sit   See *set, sit.*

site, cite   See *cite, site.*

somebody, someone, something   See pages 25–26 and 37.

suppose to   Write *supposed to.*

sure and   *Sure and* is nonstandard for *sure to. Be sure to* (not *sure and*) *bring a gift to the host.*

take   See *bring, take.*

than, then   *Than* is a conjunction used in comparisons; *then* is an adverb denoting time. *That pizza is more than I can eat. Tom laughed, and then we recognized him.*

that   See *who, which, that.*

that, which   Many writers reserve *that* for restrictive clauses, *which* for nonrestrictive clauses. (See p. 67.)

theirselves   *Theirselves* is nonstandard for *themselves.*

them   The use of *them* in place of *those* is nonstandard. *Please send those* (not *them*) *letters to the sponsors.*

then   See *than, then.*

there, their, they're   *There* is an adverb specifying place; it is also an expletive. Adverb: *Sylvia is lying there unconscious.* Expletive: *There are two plums left. Their* is a possessive pronoun. *Fred and Jane finally washed their car. They're* is a contraction of *they are. Surprisingly, they're late today.*

to, too, two   *To* is a preposition; *too* is an adverb; *two* is a number. *Too many of your shots slice to the left, but the last two were right on the mark.*

toward, towards   *Toward* and *towards* are generally interchangeable, although *toward* is preferred.

try and   *Try and* is nonstandard for *try to. I will try to* (not *try and*) *be better about writing to you.*

unique   See pages 47–48.

use to   Write *used to.*

utilize   *Utilize* means "to make use of." It often sounds pretentious; in most cases, *use* is sufficient. *I used* (not *utilized*) *the best workers to get the job done fast.*

wait for, wait on   *Wait for* means "to be in readiness for" or "await." *Wait on* means "to serve." *We're waiting for* (not *waiting on*) *Ruth before we can leave.*

ways   *Ways* is colloquial when used in place of *way* to mean "distance." *The city is a long way* (not *ways*) *from here.*

weather, whether   The noun *weather* refers to the state of the atmosphere. *Whether* is a conjunction referring to a choice between alternatives. *We wondered whether the weather would clear up in time for our picnic.*

well, good   See page 45.

where   Do not use *where* in place of *that. I heard that* (not *where*) *the crime rate is increasing.*

which   See *that, which* and *who, which, that.*

while   Avoid using *while* to mean "although" or "whereas" if there is any chance of ambiguity. *Although* (not *While*) *Gloria lost money in the slot machine, Tom won it at roulette.* Here *While* could mean either "although" or "at the same time that."

who, which, that   Use *who,* not *which,* to refer to persons. Generally, use *that* to refer to things or, occasionally, to a group or class of people. *Fans wondered how an old man who* (not *that* or *which*) *walked with a limp could play football. The team that scores the most points in this game will win the tournament.*

who, whom   See section 12d.

who's, whose   *Who's* is a contraction of *who is; whose* is a possessive pronoun. *Who's ready for more popcorn? Whose coat is this?*

would of   *Would of* is nonstandard for *would have.*

you   See page 40.

your, you're   *Your* is a possessive pronoun; *you're* is a contraction of *you are. Is that your new motorcycle? You're on the list of finalists.*

45   Glossary of grammatical terms

This glossary gives definitions for parts of speech, such as nouns; parts of sentences, such as subjects; and types of sentences, clauses, and phrases.

If you are looking up the name of an error (sentence fragment, for example), consult the index or the table of contents instead.

absolute phrase   A word group that modifies a whole clause or sentence, usually consisting of a noun followed by a participle or participial phrase: *His tone suggesting no hint of humor,* the minister told us to love our enemies because it would drive them nuts.

active vs. passive voice   When a verb is in the active voice, the subject of the sentence does the action: *The early bird catches* the early worm. In the passive voice, the subject receives the action: *The early worm is* sometimes *caught* by the early bird. Often the actor does not appear in the passive-voice sentence: *The early worm is* sometimes *caught.* (See also section 2.)

adjective   A word used to modify (describe) a noun or pronoun: the *lame* dog, *rare old* stamps, *sixteen* candles. Adjectives usually answer one of these questions: Which one? What kind of? How many or how much? (See also section 13.)

adjective clause   A subordinate clause that modifies a noun or pronoun. An adjective clause begins with a relative pronoun (*who, whom, whose, which, that*) or a relative adverb (*when, where*) and usually appears right after the word it modifies: The arrow *that has left the bow* never returns.

adverb   A word used to modify a verb, an adjective, or another adverb: rides *smoothly, unusually* attractive, *very* slowly. An adverb usually answers one of these questions: When? Where? How? Why? Under what conditions? To what degree? (See also section 13.)

adverb clause   A subordinate clause that modifies a verb (or occasionally an adjective or adverb). An adverb clause begins with a subordinating conjunction such as *although, because, if, unless,* or *when* and usually appears at the beginning or the end of a sentence: *When the well is dry,* we know the worth of water. Don't talk *unless you can improve the silence.*

agreement   See sections 10 and 12.

antecedent   A noun or pronoun to which a pronoun refers: When the *wheel* squeaks, *it* is greased. *Wheel* is the antecedent of the pronoun *it.*

appositive   A noun or noun phrase that renames a nearby noun or pronoun: Politicians, *acrobats at heart,* can lean on both sides of an issue at once.

article   The word *a, an, the,* used to mark a noun. (See also 16a.)

case   See sections 12c and 12d.

clause   A word group containing a subject, a verb, and any objects, complements, or modifiers of the verb. See *independent clause, subordinate clause.*

collective noun   See sections 10e and 12a.

common noun   See section 22a.

complement   See *subject complement, object complement.*

complex sentence   A sentence consisting of one independent clause and one or more subordinate clauses. In the following example, the subordinate clause is italicized: Do not insult the mother alligator *until you have crossed the river.*

compound-complex sentence   A sentence consisting of at least two independent clauses and at least one subordinate clause. In the following example, the subordinate clauses are italicized: Tell me *what you eat,* and I will tell you *what you are.*

compound sentence   A sentence consisting of two independent clauses. The clauses are usually joined by a comma and a coordinating conjunction (*and, but, or, nor, for, so, yet*) or by a semicolon: One arrow is easily broken, but you can't break a bundle of ten. Love is blind; envy has its eyes wide open.

conjunction   A joining word. See *coordinating conjunction, correlative conjunction, subordinating conjunction, conjunctive adverb.*

conjunctive adverb   An adverb used with a semicolon to connect independent clauses: If an animal does something, we call it instinct; *however,* if we do the same thing, we call it intelligence. The most commonly used conjunctive adverbs are *consequently, furthermore, however, moreover, nevertheless, then, therefore,* and *thus.* See page 73 for a more complete list.

coordinating conjunction   One of the following words, used to join elements of equal grammatical rank: *and, but, or, nor, for, so, yet.*

correlative conjunction   A pair of conjunctions connecting grammatically equal elements: *either . . . or, neither . . . nor, whether . . . or, not only . . . but also,* and *both . . . and.*

count nouns   See page 55.

demonstrative pronoun   A pronoun used to identify or point to a noun: *this, that, these, those. This* hanging will surely be a lesson to me.

direct object   A word or word group that receives the action of the verb: The little snake studies *the ways of the big serpent.* The complete direct object is *the ways of the big serpent.* The simple direct object is always a noun or pronoun, such as *ways.*

expletive   The word *there* or *it* when used at the beginning of a sentence to delay the subject: *There* are many paths to the top of the mountain. *It* is not good to wake a sleeping lion. The delayed subjects are the noun *paths* and the infinitive phrase *to wake a sleeping lion.*

gerund   A verb form ending in *-ing,* used as a noun: Continual *dripping* wears away a stone. *Dripping* is used as the subject of the verb *wears away.*

gerund phrase   A gerund and its objects, complements, or modifiers. A gerund phrase always functions as a noun, usually as a subject, a subject complement, or a direct object. In the following example, the phrase functions as a subject: *Justifying a fault* doubles it.

helping verb   One of the following words, when used with a main verb: *be, am, is, are, was, were, being, been; has, have, had; do, does, did; can, will, shall, should, could, would, may, might, must.* Helping verbs always precede main verbs: *will work, is working, had worked.*

indefinite pronoun   A pronoun that refers to a nonspecific person or thing: *Anyone* who serves God for money will serve the Devil for better wages. The most common indefinite pronouns are *all, another, any, anybody, anyone, anything, both, each, either, everybody, everyone, everything, few, many, neither, nobody, none, no one, nothing, one, some, somebody, someone, something.*

independent clause A clause (containing a subject and a verb) that can or does stand alone as a sentence. Every sentence consists of at least one independent clause. In addition, many sentences contain subordinate clauses that function as adjectives, adverbs, or nouns. See also *subordinate clause.*

indirect object A noun or pronoun that names to whom or for whom the action is done: Fate gives *us* our relatives. An indirect object always precedes a direct object, in this case *our relatives.*

infinitive The word *to* followed by a verb: *to think, to dream.*

infinitive phrase An infinitive and its objects, complements, or modifiers. An infinitive phrase can function as a noun, an adjective, or an adverb: *To side with truth* is noble. We do not have the right *to abandon the poor.* Do not use a hatchet *to remove a fly from your friend's forehead.*

intensive or reflexive pronoun A pronoun ending in *-self: myself, yourself, himself, herself, itself, ourselves, yourselves, themselves.* An intensive pronoun emphasizes a noun or another pronoun: I *myself* don't understand my moods. A reflexive pronoun names a receiver of an action identical with the doer of the action: Did you cut *yourself*?

interjection A word expressing surprise or emotion: *Oh! Wow! Hey! Hooray!*

interrogative pronoun A pronoun used to open a question: *who, whom, whose, which, what. What* does history teach us?

intransitive verb See *transitive and intransitive verbs.*

irregular verb See *regular and irregular verbs.* Or see section 11a.

linking verb A verb that links a subject to a subject complement, a word or word group that renames or describes the subject: Prejudice *is* the child of ignorance. Good medicine sometimes *tastes* bitter. The most common linking verbs are forms of *be: be, am, is, are, was, were, being, been.* The following verbs sometimes function as linking verbs: *appear, become, feel, grow, look, make, seem, smell, sound, taste.*

modifier A word, phrase, or clause that describes or qualifies the meaning of a word. Modifiers include adjectives, adverbs, prepositional phrases, participial phrases, some infinitive phrases, and adjective and adverb clauses.

mood See section 11c.

noncount noun See page 56.

noun The name of a person, place, or thing: The *cat* in *gloves* catches no *mice*.

noun clause A subordinate clause that functions as a noun, usually as a subject, a subject complement, or a direct object. In the following sentence, the italicized noun clauses function as subject and subject complement: *What history teaches us* is *that we have never learned anything from it*. Noun clauses usually begin with *how, who, whom, that, what, whether,* or *why*.

noun equivalent A word or word group that functions like a noun: a pronoun, a noun and its modifiers, a gerund phrase, some infinitive phrases, a noun clause.

object See *direct object, indirect object*.

object complement A word or word group that renames or describes a direct object. It always appears after the direct object: Our fears do make us *traitors*. Love makes all hard hearts *gentle*.

object of a preposition See *prepositional phrase*.

participial phrase A present or past participle and its objects, complements, or modifiers. A participial phrase always functions as an adjective describing a noun or pronoun. Usually it appears before or after the word it modifies: *Being weak,* foxes are distinguished by superior tact. Truth *kept in the dark* will never save the world.

participle, past A verb form usually ending in *-d, -ed, -n, -en,* or *-t: asked, spoken, stolen*. Although past participles usually function as main verbs (was *asked,* had *spoken*), they may also be used as adjectives (the *stolen* car).

participle, present A verb form ending in *-ing*. Although present participles usually function as main verbs (is *rising*), they may also be used as adjectives (the *rising* tide).

parts of speech A system for classifying words. Many words can function as more than one part of speech. See *noun, pronoun, verb, adjective, adverb, preposition, conjunction, interjection*.

passive voice See *active vs. passive voice*.

personal pronoun One of the following pronouns, used to refer to a specific person or thing: *I, me, you, she, her, he,* *him, it, we, us, they, them.* Admonish your friends in private; praise *them* in public.

phrase   A word group that lacks a subject, a verb, or both. Most phrases function within sentences as adjectives, as adverbs, or as nouns. See *absolute phrase, appositive, gerund phrase, infinitive phrase, participial phrase, prepositional phrase.*

possessive case   See section 19a.

possessive pronoun   A pronoun used to indicate ownership: *my, mine, your, yours, her, hers, his, its, our, ours, your, yours, their, theirs.* A cock has great influence on *his* own dunghill.

predicate   A verb and any objects, complements, and modifiers that go with it: A clean glove *often hides a dirty hand.*

preposition   A word placed before a noun or noun equivalent to form a phrase modifying another word in the sentence. The preposition indicates the relation between the noun (or noun equivalent) and the word the phrase modifies. The most common prepositions are *about, above, across, after, against, along, among, around, at, before, behind, below, beside, besides, between, beyond, by, down, during, except, for, from, in, inside, into, like, near, next, of, off, on, onto, out, outside, over, past, since, than, through, to, toward, under, unlike, until, up, with,* and *without.*

prepositional phrase   A phrase beginning with a preposition and ending with a noun or noun equivalent (called the *object of the preposition*). Most prepositional phrases function as adjectives or adverbs. Adjective phrases usually come right after the noun or pronoun they modify: Variety is the spice *of life.* Adverb phrases usually appear at the beginning or the end of the sentence: *To the ant,* a few drops of rain are a flood. Do not judge a tree *by its bark.*

progressive verb forms   See page 34.

pronoun   A word used in place of a noun. Usually the pronoun substitutes for a specific noun, known as its antecedent. In the following example, *elephant* is the antecedent of the pronoun *him:* When an *elephant* is in trouble, even a frog will kick *him.* See also *demonstrative pronoun, indefinite pronoun, intensive or reflexive pronoun, interrogative pronoun, personal pronoun, possessive pronoun, relative pronoun.*

proper noun   See pages 88–89.

regular and irregular verbs   When a verb is regular, both the past tense and past participle are formed by adding *-ed* or *-d* to the base form of the word: *walk, walked, walked.*

Irregular verbs are formed in a variety of other ways: *ride, rode, ridden; begin, began, begun; go, went, gone;* and so on. See also 11a.

relative adverb   The word *when* or *where,* when used to introduce an adjective clause.

relative pronoun   One of the following words, when used to introduce an adjective clause: *who, whom, whose, which, that.* A fable is a bridge *that* leads to truth.

sentence   A word group consisting of at least one independent clause. See *also simple sentence, compound sentence, complex sentence, compound-complex sentence.*

simple sentence   A sentence consisting of one independent clause and no subordinate clauses: The frog in the well knows nothing of the ocean.

subject   A word or word group that names who or what the sentence is about. In the following example, the complete subject (the simple subject and all of its modifiers) is italicized: *Historical books that contain no lies* are tedious. The simple subject is *books.* See also *subject after verb, understood subject.*

subject after verb   Although the subject normally precedes the verb, sentences are sometimes inverted. In the following example, the subject *the real tinsel* comes after the verb *lies:* Behind the phony tinsel of Hollywood lies the real tinsel. When a sentence begins with the expletive *there* or *it,* the subject always follows the verb. See *expletive.*

subject complement   A word or word group that follows a linking verb and either renames or describes the subject of the sentence. If the subject complement renames the subject, it is a noun or a noun equivalent: The handwriting on the wall may be *a forgery.* If it describes the subject, it is an adjective: Love is *blind.*

subjunctive mood   See section 11c.

subordinate clause   A clause (containing a subject and verb) that cannot stand alone as a sentence. Subordinate clauses function within sentences as adjectives, adverbs, or nouns. They begin with subordinating conjuctions such as *although, because, if,* and *until* or with relative pronouns such as *who, which,* and *that.* See *adjective clause, adverb clause, noun clause.*

subordinating conjunction   A word that introduces a subordinate clause and indicates its relation to the rest of the sentence. The most common subordinating conjunctions are *after, although, as, as if, because, before, even though, if, since, so that, than, that, though, unless, until, when,* *where, whether,* and *while.* Note: The relative pronouns *who, whom, whose, which,* and *that* also introduce subordinate clauses.

tenses   See section 11b.

transitive and intransitive verbs   Transitive verbs take direct objects, nouns or noun equivalents that receive the action. In the following example, the transitive verb *loves* takes the direct object *its mother:* A spoiled child never *loves* its mother. Intransitive verbs do not take direct objects: Money *talks.* If any words follow an intransitive verb, they are adverbs or word groups functioning as adverbs: The sun *will set* without your assistance.

understood subject   The subject *you* when it is understood but not actually present in the sentence. Understood subjects occur in sentences that issue commands or advice: [*You*] Hitch your wagon to a star.

verb   A word that expresses action (*jump, think*) or being (*is, was*). A sentence's verb is composed of a main verb possibly preceded by one or more helping verbs: The best fish *swim* near the bottom. A marriage *is* not *built* in a day. Verbs have five forms: the base form, or dictionary form (*walk, ride*); the past-tense form (*walked, rode*); the past participle (*walked, ridden*); the present participle (*walking, riding*); and the *-s* form (*walks, rides*).

verbal phrase   See *gerund phrase, infinitive phrase, participial phrase.*

A List of Style Manuals

A Pocket Style Manual describes three commonly used systems of documentation: MLA, used in English and the humanities (see section 32); APA, used in psychology and the social sciences (see section 37); and *Chicago*, used primarily in history (see section 42). Following is a list of style manuals used in a variety of disciplines.

BIOLOGY (See dianahacker.com/resdoc for more information.)

Council of Biology Editors. *Scientific Style and Format: The CBE Manual for Authors, Editors, and Publishers.* 6th ed. New York: Cambridge UP, 1994.

BUSINESS

American Management Association. *The AMA Style Guide for Business Writing.* New York: AMACOM, 1996.

CHEMISTRY

Dodd, Janet S., ed. *The ACS Style Guide: A Manual for Authors and Editors.* 2nd ed. Washington: Amer. Chemical Soc., 1997.

ENGLISH AND THE HUMANITIES (See section 32.)

Gibaldi, Joseph. *MLA Handbook for Writers of Research Papers.* 6th ed. New York: MLA, 2003.

GEOLOGY

Bates, Robert L., Rex Buchanan, and Marla Adkins-Heljeson, eds. *Geowriting: A Guide to Writing, Editing, and Printing in Earth Science.* 5th ed. Alexandria: Amer. Geological Inst., 1995.

GOVERNMENT DOCUMENTS

Garner, Diane L. *The Complete Guide to Citing Government Information Resources: A Manual for Writers and Librarians.* Rev. ed. Bethesda: Congressional Information Service, 1993.

United States Government Printing Office. *Style Manual.* Washington: GPO, 2000.

HISTORY (See section 42.)

The Chicago Manual of Style. 15th ed. Chicago: U of Chicago P, 2003.

JOURNALISM

Goldstein, Norm, ed. *Associated Press Stylebook and Briefing on Media Law.* 35th ed. New York: Associated Press, 2000.

LAW

Harvard Law Review et al. *The Bluebook: A Uniform System of Citation.* 17th ed. Cambridge: Harvard Law Rev. Assn., 2000.

LINGUISTICS

Linguistic Society of America. "LSA Style Sheet." Published annually in the December issue of the *LSA Bulletin.*

MATHEMATICS

American Mathematical Society. *The AMS Author Handbook: General Instructions for Preparing Manuscripts.* Rev. ed. Providence: AMS, 1996.

MEDICINE

Iverson, Cheryl, et al. *American Medical Association Manual of Style: A Guide for Authors and Editors.* 9th ed. Baltimore: Williams, 1998.

MUSIC

Holoman, D. Kern, ed. *Writing about Music: A Style Sheet from the Editors of* 19th-Century Music. Berkeley: U of California P, 1988.

PHYSICS

American Institute of Physics. *Style Manual: Instructions to Authors and Volume Editors for the Preparation of AIP Book Manuscripts.* 5th ed. New York: AIP, 1995.

POLITICAL SCIENCE

American Political Science Association. *Style Manual for Political Science.* Rev. ed. Washington: Amer. Political Science Assn., 1993.

PSYCHOLOGY AND THE SOCIAL SCIENCES (See section 37.)

American Psychological Association. *Publication Manual of the American Psychological Association.* 5th ed. Washington: APA, 2001.

SCIENCE AND TECHNICAL WRITING

American National Standard for the Preparation of Scientific Papers for Written or Oral Presentation. New York: Amer. Natl. Standards Inst., 1979.

Microsoft Corporation. *Microsoft Manual of Style for Technical Publications.* Redmond: Microsoft, 1998.

Rubens, Philip, ed. *Science and Technical Writing: A Manual of Style.* 2nd ed. New York: Routledge, 2001.

SOCIAL WORK

National Association of Social Workers. *Writing for the NASW Press: Information for Authors.* Rev. ed. Washington: Natl. Assn. of Social Workers, 1995.

Index

Checklist for Global Revisions

Focus

▶ Is the thesis stated clearly enough? Is it placed where readers will notice it?

▶ Does each idea support the thesis?

Organization

▶ Can readers easily follow the structure? Would headings help?

▶ Do topic sentences signal new ideas?

▶ Are ideas presented in a logical order?

Content

▶ Is the supporting material persuasive?

▶ Are important ideas fully developed?

▶ Is the draft concise enough—free of irrelevant or repetitious material?

▶ Are the parts proportioned sensibly? Do major ideas receive enough attention?

Style

▶ Is the voice appropriate—not too stuffy, not too breezy?

▶ Are the sentences clear, emphatic, and varied?

Use of Quotations

▶ Is quoted material introduced with a signal phrase and documented with a citation?

▶ Is quoted material enclosed within quotation marks (unless it has been set off from the text)?

▶ Is each quotation word-for-word accurate? If not, do brackets or ellipsis dots mark the changes or omissions?

Use of Other Source Material

▶ Is the draft free of plagiarism? Are summaries and paraphrases written in the writer's own words—not copied or half-copied from the source?

▶ Has source material that is not common knowledge been documented?

Revision Symbols

abbr	abbreviation **23a**	" "	quotation marks **20**
ad	adverb or adjective **13**	.	period **21a**
add	add needed word **4**	?	question mark **21b**
agr	agreement **10, 12a**	!	exclamation point **21c**
appr	inappropriate language **9**	—	dash **21d**
art	article **16a**	( )	parentheses **21e**
awk	awkward	[ ]	brackets **21f**
cap	capital letter **22**	. . .	ellipsis mark **21g**
case	case **12c, 12d**	/	slash **21h**
cs	comma splice **15**	*pass*	ineffective passive **2, 11d**
dm	dangling modifier **7c**	*pn agr*	pronoun agreement **12a**
-ed	*-ed* ending **11a**	*ref*	pronoun reference **12b**
ESL	English as a second language **16**	*run-on*	run-on sentence **15**
frag	sentence fragment **14**	*-s*	*-s* ending on verb **10, 16b**
fs	fused sentence **15**	*sexist*	sexist language **9c, 12a**
hyph	hyphen **24b**	*shift*	confusing shift **5**
irreg	irregular verb **11a**	*sl*	slang **9b**
ital	italics (underlining) **23c**	*sp*	misspelled word **24a**
jarg	jargon **9a**	*sv agr*	subject-verb agreement **10**
lc	use lowercase letter **22**	*t*	verb tense **11b**
mix	mixed construction **6**	*usage*	see Glossary of Usage
mm	misplaced modifier **7a–b, 7d**	*v*	voice **2, 11d**
mood	mood **11c**	*var*	sentence variety **8**
num	numbers **23b**	*vb*	problem with verb **11, 16b–c**
om	omitted word **4, 16a, 16c**	*w*	wordy **1**
p	punctuation	*//*	faulty parallelism **3**
ˆ	comma **17a–i**	∧	insert
no ,	no comma **17j**	x	obvious error
;	semicolon **18a**	#	insert space
:	colon **18b**	⌒	close up space
ˇ	apostrophe **19**		

Contents

dianahacker.com/pocket

Expert advice for writing in *all* ▮▮▮▮▮▮▮ Whether
you're writing for histo▮▮▮▮▮▮▮▮▮▮▮▮▮▮▮▮ erature,
women's studies, or ▮▮▮▮▮▮▮▮▮▮▮▮▮▮▮▮ ll find *A
Pocket Style Manual* a ▮▮▮▮▮▮▮rd, practical reference
to the essentials of wr▮▮▮g and research. The book's
companion Web site now provides comprehensive online
support for strengthening writing and editing skills and
for using and documenting sources.

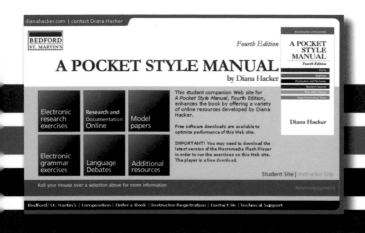

BEDFORD/ST. MARTIN'S
bedfordstmartins.com

ISBN 0-312-40684-3

9 780312 406844